FASSBINDER

Edited by Tony Rayns

Revised and expanded edition

1980

General Editor David Wilson

Published by/British Film Institute/127 Charing Cross Road, London WC2H 0EA

For Barbara and David Stone

Acknowledgments

Numerous people have generously assisted with the preparation of the first and second editions of the book. The editor and authors would particularly like to thank the following: Ian Christie, Gillian Hartnoll and David Meeker of the BFI; Christoph Schlotterer of Carl Hanser Verlag; Scilla Alvarado, Ian Bodenham, Richard Collins, Jan Dawson, Frieda Grafe, Sheila Lattimore and Enno Patalas. Special thanks to Hans Helmut Prinzler for providing information for the filmography and bibliography.

Copyright © 1976, 1979 British Film Institute
Making an Impact – Rainer Werner Fassbinder and the Theatre by Peter Iden (from *Reihe Film 2: Rainer Werner Fassbinder*, edited by Peter W. Jansen and Wolfram Schütte) © 1974 Carl Hanser Verlag, Munich.

First edition, 1976
Reprinted, 1977
Second edition, 1979

ISBN 0 85170 095 0 (hardcover)
ISBN 0 85170 096 9 (paperback)

Contents

Introduction to the Second Edition Tony Rayns	v
The Postwar German Cinema Thomas Elsaesser	1
Making an Impact – Fassbinder and the Theatre Peter Iden	17
A Cinema of Vicious Circles (and Afterword) Thomas Elsaesser	24
Reading Fassbinder's Sexual Politics Richard Dyer	54
Memories of Fassbinder's TV Work Thomas Thieringer	65
Eight Hours are not a Day (and Afterword) Manuel Alvarado	70
Fassbinder, Form and Syntax Tony Rayns	79
Five Interviews with Fassbinder Christian Braad Thomsen	82
Documentation Tony Rayns	102

Introduction to the Second Edition

Tony Rayns

The first edition of this book – written, in the main, four years ago – announced itself as an attempt to confront the discrepancy between Fassbinder's status at home in West Germany and his status abroad. On the one side, a relentless bombardment of various sectors of the public with productions in at least four 'popular' media, frequently generating scandal or controversy in the process. On the other, a scattering of subtitled 'art' movies, attracting reflex-auteurist acclaim or dismissal. The book's strategy was to elucidate the political, social, economic, cultural and aesthetic circumstances that produced Fassbinder. In other words, to analyse the chief determinants behind the films, thereby clearing the ground for an appraisal of the value (or otherwise) of Fassbinder's work to a 'progressive' European film culture.

The aim of this second edition remains substantially the same. The materials gathered on the following pages are disparate in method, scope and aesthetic orientation. They are brought together with the primary intention of *informing* the reader; there is no attempt at close textual criticism, and very little analysis of individual films. The Biography, Filmography and Bibliography have been updated to January 1979 (when Fassbinder was completing the shooting of his thirty-fourth feature, *The Third Generation*); the interview section has been greatly expanded; new essays by Richard Dyer and Thomas Thieringer have been added; one essay has been completely rewritten, and new Afterwords have been added to two others.

The book's relatively unchanged emphasis reflects no complacency on the part of the editor or the authors. On the contrary, it is apparent that theoretical and semantic analyses of Fassbinder's 'pre-ideological', 'naive' melodramas are overdue. Recent years have seen Fassbinder attacked not only by the bourgeois establishment but also by groups who would see themselves as anti-bourgeois: feminists, gay activists and 'psychoanalytical' critics like Serge Daney in *Cahiers du cinéma*. Many of these attacks (like those prompted by the supposed anti-semitism of Fassbinder's unproduced play *The Garbage, The City and Death* and its film adaptation *Shadow of Angels*) have been instances of factions 'obediently' rising to the bait of Fassbinder's provocations – as if *Martha*, for instance, were not *designed* to outrage feminists. Some of the following essays examine the role of 'the provocation' in Fassbinder's movies, plays and 'public image', and go some way towards accounting for it. But there is still an urgent need for a sustained theorisation of Fassbinder's strategies, aesthetic and 'political'.

Why, then, can such a theorisation not be found in this book? There are three main reasons.

(1) There is still a considerable problem of access outside West Germany to Fassbinder's work. A few of the early (pre-1971) films have come into distribution in Britain and America, and retrospectives have been mounted at the Pacific Film Archive in Berkeley and the National Film Theatre in London. These welcome developments, however, can scarcely intimate the sheer intensity of Fassbinder's address to his home audience via the cinema screen, the TV screen, the printed page and the stage. The principles of tautology, repetition and permutation on which much of the work rests therefore remain hidden from those not resident in West Germany.

(2) Any work on Fassbinder at present is inherently work-in-progress. Partly because Fassbinder is not only prolific but also exceptionally versatile in adapting himself to whatever options are open to him: his sole foray to date into the territory of the 'international art film' (*Despair*) was followed almost immediately by a decisive withdrawal from that territory (*In a Year of 13 Moons*). Partly because work on Fassbinder must be predicated on work on his Hollywood models, and that work has itself barely been begun.

(3) The film cultures of Europe and America have not yet produced a sufficient body of people able and willing to undertake the work.

This last observation in no way reflects on the work of the writers who have contributed to the book as it stands. But each of them has, of necessity, worked in isolation; circumstances do not permit a rigorously unified approach. Hence the book's diversity, and its internal contradictions of method and ideology. Hence also its bias towards factual information, wherein lies the hope that the book will serve as an adequate reference source for the work that must follow.

March 1979

The Postwar German Cinema

Thomas Elsaesser

1 Introduction

British film-makers have some reason to look to West Germany with envy. Fassbinder seems only the most striking figure among a whole generation of directors who have been going from strength to strength. On the ground, the situation looks a little different. One must guard against the supposition that there is a unified group or movement. The geographical distance between Munich and Berlin, the two main film centres, also expresses a political polarisation; when Fassbinder attended the Berlin Festival in 1975, he was booed with the hot anger that indicates raw nerves and animosities dating from long-standing quarrels. The fact that Fassbinder likes to play the *enfant terrible* might explain the virulence of some of the attacks, as it singles him out as fodder for the press. But the conditions under which the new German cinema operates don't allow for more than strategic alliances; for the rest, it's 'every man for himself' as the title of Werner Herzog's Kaspar Hauser film suggests, not without topical reference. None the less, Fassbinder, Herzog, Wenders, Schroeter, Schlöndorff, Thome, Brandner and Moorse (to name a few who are 'doing their own thing') remain products of the historical and (film) political conjunction that both frustrates their work and makes it possible.

What is going on in Germany has a lesson somewhere, mainly about the conditions under which a contemporary 'independent' cinema is possible in European countries, and (by the same token) about the limits set for such a cinema in its ideological and aesthetic function. The fact that a new German cinema of feature films exists is a good sign, but it should not lead one to overlook some of its problematic and anachronistic traits. If one brackets out the historical determinants that give film-makers like Fassbinder the full measure of their success or failure, one is likely to ignore the quality of achievement or tentative exploration in their films. In many ways Fassbinder is an exception, though not in respect of the ideological conditions which his films reflect at once precisely and obliquely. The new German cinema of the late Sixties and Seventies, that cinema of which festivals and national film theatres are now taking notice, has its existence inside a field of force, a triangle made up of the German film industry, the hegemony of Hollywood over Europe, and the media policy of the Federal German government. The latter especially has thrown up contradictions, of which today's film-makers are the ambiguous beneficiaries.

2 The Film Industry: Illusions of Autonomy

The German film industry is as crisis-prone, unstable and economically unsound as that of any other European country, only more so. Compared with Britain, France or Italy, Germany's specific development makes its film industry one of the weakest in relation to its size. Low investment and capitalisation have widened the disparity (perhaps endemic in all film-making) between semi- or pre-capitalist methods of production and monopoly capitalist methods of distribution. An index of the industry's backwardness is the extremely poor unionisation: an important factor in that it allowed the 'independents' to enter the market without encountering much resistance to non-union actors and small *ad hoc* crews, keeping production at the level of manufacture and craft. The various counter-cinemas since the mid-Sixties have consistently been able to utilise this gap to their advantage, since it obliged the state to intervene in the 'free' play of market forces to help the industry survive at all.

Some of the industry's weaknesses are therefore structural, and in part date from the time when it was established as a virtual extension of the War Ministry (in late 1917 the German War Ministry together with the Deutsche Bank founded the Universum Film AG, better known as Ufa). Most of the deficiencies since World War II, however, are conjunctural: the result of West Germany's exposed ideological position as a major area of East-West confrontation. Especially incisive were the overt political and economic goals that the US pursued in building up West Germany as a capitalist stronghold to counter the Soviet sphere of influence east of the Elbe. Exigencies of the cold war accounted for much of the Allied Control Commission's policies for press, radio and film. Two priorities governed American thinking on the film industry in particular: the reinstatement of 'reliable' (if necessary, ex-Nazi) personnel in executive positions, and the necessity that the industry be organised on lines that could transmit an ideologically clear message without being sufficiently organised to achieve economic dominance. 'Information Control will provide the Germans with information which will influence them to understand and accept the US programme of occupation,' read one of the first directives relating to the mass media (April 1947); US Secretary of State Byrnes was equally unambiguous when he announced, 'What we have to do now is not to make the world safe for democracy, but to make it safe for the United States.' One of the American officers involved in the programme of film industry denazification stated that his task was in practice impossible, 'since virtually all directors, writers, actors, cameramen and technicians had been more or less active members of the NSDAP'. Consequently, they all found work again, usually in their old jobs. 40% of the directors working in the German film industry in 1960 had been 'prominent' during the Nazi era.

The economic development and political significance of the German cinema bears the scars of American policy to this day: economically, in the dispersal of production (to Berlin, Munich, temporarily Hamburg) and the chronic lack of finance that persists on the level of investment; ideologically, in that shortage of funds in turn necessitated steering measures and directives on the part of the West German government which amounted to indirect political and artistic censorship. Permanently suffering in comparisons with the Americans, the German film industry retreated into an almost exclusive orientation to the home market, a legacy from its inception that had been aggravated during the Nazi period by the state's take-over of the Ufa empire, fully integrating it into Goebbels' Ministry of Propaganda, where Hitler's economic obsession with the idea of autarchy was fully applied to film production. After World War II the isolationist orientation survived as a reflex of the industry in the ever-more-helpless struggle against Hollywood supremacy. In the Fifties, it became stated government policy to make the film industry independent of imports, and to regain for German productions the whole of the home market: not only an illusory and short-sighted aim, but also an argument adduced to silence growing criticism that the Adenauer government was simply an executive arm of the Americans, to the detriment of Germany's own bourgeoisie.

As a consequence of this home-oriented production policy, West Germany (economically strong because of its leading position in world trade) shows exceptionally poor export figures for its films, even in the relatively buoyant years of the mid-Fifties: in 1955, a total of 15,000,000 DM was earned in exports (including script rights, leasing of actors under German contracts, etc.) while 138,000,000 DM worth of films was imported. The tendency to remain something of a Bavarian cottage industry is reflected in the themes and genres: films about gynaecologists getting their patients pregnant, neo-imperialist 'Sissi' films dreaming of Viennese pastry and Hapsburg glories, the Bavarian mountain musicals, the beer-mug and lederhosen comedies. They have made few friends for the German post-war cinema abroad, and it is noticeable that some of the films from younger directors still have an air of provincialism and other-worldliness, even if today this constitutes for many foreigners their charm, their 'identity'. A film like Fassbinder's *Katzelmacher* must seem quaint to a European public, but a German audience will recognise the sardonic (albeit lovingly recalled) memories of the *'Heimatfilm'*.

Another effect of catering for a home market only was the impression of drabness that German films so often convey. Since it could not hope to produce for export, the industry hardly ever undertook to make expensive films. (Fritz Lang once joked that he ruined Ufa and precipitated the Nazi take-over with *Metropolis,* Germany's first – and last – all-out attempt to beat the Americans, a gamble which did not pay off.) Volker Schlöndorff, one of the few 'new' German directors to have any experience in international co-productions (he directed *Michael Kohlhaas,* a German/American/Czech co-production), criticises the industry for its timidity: 'It simply makes good sense for a film industry to undertake three or four times a year projects which cost 5 or 8 million DM, because that way a large number of technicians and other people are employed and trained, it's a healthy shot in the arm for the industry itself. The Italians and the French are very clever to produce something like *Borsalino* once in a while, which not only raises the industry's infrastructure to the latest stage of technology, but can also be used to break into the world market: in its wake, they can sell a Truffaut or a Chabrol, and that way the notion of the "French film" gets international currency two or three times a year. If France produced only Truffaut or Chabrol films, it couldn't export films at all. That's one of the things that's been wrong with the German film industry ever since the Fifties. One always started from the assumption that a film had to earn 80 or 90% of its money at home.' Schlöndorff knows that such an extreme 'commercial' argument is not shared by many of his colleagues, but it is true that so long as entertainment quality and production values are low, a vicious circle sets in: not only can German films not compete in the international market, but they also look shoddy in the home market compared with Hollywood glamour. But since the Americans' various decartelisation laws after the war had ensured that no centralised industry could emerge from the process of dismantling the still considerable Ufa holdings (thus eliminating a potential German rival to their monopoly position), the film industry remained an unattractive object of investment as long as profits were high in other sectors of Germany's post-war boom economy.

What the Americans had supported in 1945/6 was the rebuilding of the cinemas and the distribution sector; the latter was first in the hands of the Allied powers (mainly America and Britain), but soon sold to German firms. However, the only distributors able to weather the various crises (1953, 1961) were those with links with the American majors, and today there is only one major distributor (Constantin) who is not American-owned. The late Forties policy of favouring distributors while only reluctantly granting licences to producers unbalanced the relation between production and distribution in the years to come, making the latter strong at the expense of the former. The many small independent producers who tried to establish themselves in the early Fifties were – not unlike today – a promising start for a new film culture, but because they were never financially viable and were prevented by law from merging, they usually collapsed after one or two films. Of the 102 production companies registered in 1954, more than 70 had a basic working capital of less than 20,000 DM. Another circumstance nipped West German production in the bud: the MPEA (Motion Picture Export Association) had been able to put pressure on the American government to veto any West German legislation that might have imposed quota restrictions on the import of American films. Since many of the Hollywood imports dated from the Forties and had already paid their way in America and Britain, they could be offered to the cinemas at rates that undercut new West German productions. Dumping was also practised by German distributors, who re-released scores of Nazi entertainment films from the Thirties and Forties, also at rates with which new films could not compete.

The major recession in audience demand hit Germany in the late Fifties: the introduction of TV and the increasing availability of private cars changed patterns of leisure activity as drastically as elsewhere in Europe and America, and cinema admissions dropped from an all-time high in 1956 of 900 million to an eventual 192 million in 1968. German productions were worst hit by this decline, while the Americans were able to 'export' their own crisis through domestic cut-backs and runaway productions. That the German film industry was increasingly operating at a loss can be seen from the fact that in 1967 German films accounted for 40% of the films on offer, but represented only 24% of the market in terms of box-office gross. In the early Sixties, the film industry was already run down to the point where the Americans preferred to invest in Britain or Italy rather than in Germany: they controlled the German market directly through distribution, and since the MPEA had succeeded in their aim to 'secure absolute freedom of movement for American films' (i.e., no profits from distribution were frozen in Germany, as they were in Britain and France), American companies had little incentive to invest in Germany's industry by acquiring studios. German co-productions were mainly with American subsidiaries in France and Italy, or with filmically 'underdeveloped' countries like Yugoslavia and Spain.

The only option that German film production had for staying alive was to appeal to the government for credits and subsidies. And the record of these state interventions, the unsuccessful role that successive governments played by mediating between purely economic, directly ideological and 'cultural' objectives, provides the major premise for the economic base of the new and newest German cinemas.

3 Government Intervention: Sponsorship or Censorship?

In line with its contradictory position of executing the wishes of the Americans while holding the interests of its own bourgeoisie as its mandate, the CDU government decided as early as 1950 to make available to the industry so-called guaranteed credits *(Ausfallbürgschaften)*; the government guaranteed the banks the credits they gave to distributors, who in turn advanced a distribution guarantee to the producers. The intention was to encourage small producers to raise money for films, but the actual effect was not at all encouraging: the system of passing the buck was administratively cumbersome, it tripled the producers' dependencies, and, in the final instance, brought film-making under the direct control and censorship of the state. Scripts, contracts, shooting schedules and production estimates down to the last detail had to be approved by a board of state-appointed trustees (the so-called *Revisions und Treuhandgesellschaft)*, who also had the right to block funds for productions already under way if recommendations were not implemented. After only two years the system had to be modified, not only because of financial losses, but also because the industry's own organisation, the SPIO *(Spitzenorganisation der Deutschen Filmwirtschaft),* protested against the unacceptable level of interference: 'We note with growing concern that ... the era of guaranteed credits ... stands under the sign of government control, which makes film production into the executive organ of an apparatus directly dependent on the state.'

The 1952 modifications, however, had even more disastrous effects. They removed the last vestiges of support for a 'pluralistic' film production and reversed the anti-trust implications of the original credits: henceforth only producers who promised a package deal (usually eight films in a row) could apply for guaranteed credits. Right away, this limited money to those who already had a dominant position in the market. For most producers, a programme of eight films was well beyond their capacities: they died either a slow death of financial asphyxiation or a fast one by overcommitting themselves and going bankrupt. None of the companies which accepted credits under these terms survived into the Sixties; they were tempted into speculation, any long-term investment or production policy was subverted by the volatile situation of an artificially stoked production boom, and the market was flooded with films that killed each other like weeds in an untended garden. 1955 was a major boom year (120 films compared with 84 in 1954) because it became known that the government was to stop credits altogether, and there was a rush to get in at the last minute.

By 1956 the industry had experienced another shift of power, this time in the distributors' favour: they had formed their own companies to produce the required eight films, for they alone were able to exploit them in the cinemas. The guaranteed credits had actively encouraged a monopoly situation in the market, but in the process had destroyed the economic initiative and independence of the producing sector. The concentration of capital that took place meant that a handful of people held most of the key positions (Arthur Brauner of CCC, Waldfried Barthel of Constantin and Ilse and Walter Kubaschewski of Gloria were the movie moguls of the Fifties), transforming the industry into a closed shop where one form or another of nepotism determined the chances of entry.

In fact, the government had already swung over to a pro-monopolist film policy in 1953 when, in a hurried undercover action, it had tried to prevent the Americans from selling the old Ufa holdings to individual bidders, by asking the Deutsche Bank – history repeating itself ominously – to form three separate companies to develop the various assets of the former state company. In 1956 the three firms were openly reunited as a consortium headed by the Deutsche Bank and the Dresdner Bank. The new production-cum-theatre-chain giant turned out to be a dinosaur. It came too late to combat American supremacy, and its organisational structure was already anachronistic at its inception. In 1961, the second major crisis year, Ufa collapsed and most of its assets were liquidated. Once again, government interference had brought the kiss of death to an autonomous German cinema. It simply aggravated the internal contradictions of the industry as a whole.

After the guaranteed credits were scrapped, a scramble for subsidies via tax relief began. Mindful of the poor reputation and quality of German cinema, however, the government administered tax relief indirectly. An institution that had hitherto existed at individual federal state level was centralised in 1955, becoming the FBW *(Filmbewertungstelle Wiesbaden);* its purpose was to award quality ratings to films of 'artistic merit' (*wertvoll* – valuable, or *besonders wertvoll* – especially valuable). A film with a quality rating was entitled to considerable relief from entertainment tax at the box office, which meant that it showed a profit for the distributor on less real revenue. Given the low returns on even successful German films, a quality rating often decided whether a film was to be distributed at all. The so-called 'quality' incentive worked as an additional means of censorship, economically penalising politically inopportune films. Straub's *Chronicle of Anna Magdalena Bach,* for example, had to fight a long and much-publicised battle to get a rating at all. Since ministerial or local civil servants made up 40% of the FBW membership, the state had a massive share of the vote that determined filmic 'quality'. De facto, the incentive functioned as an actual disincentive to producers and directors to tackle 'difficult' subjects. Instead of quality and experiment, it encouraged mediocrity and conformism.

The ratings were of economic significance only as long as the federal states continued to tax films. With the deteriorating market, entertainment tax was gradually reduced, and the FBW's function dwindled accordingly, until it was given a new prominence in 1967 with the introduction of the Film Subsidies Bill *(Filmförderungsgesetz).* The intervening period, between 1962 and 1967, saw the decisive struggles for a new German cinema. The Bill not only revealed the dilapidation of the established film industry, but also gave prominence to another sort of subsidy altogether, which in subsequent years has tended to displace the combat zone from the film industry itself to the shadowy domain of 'culture'.

One of the peculiarities of the German federal system is that affairs of culture and education are under the jurisdiction of the individual states rather than the federal government. Yet it clearly makes no sense to encourage a 'regional' film industry. The federal government's interventions were limited to direct economic measures, like the guaranteed credits and the botched Ufa merger. Entertainment tax and quality ratings remain matters for the states to administer. The only level at which a federal initiative does not violate the sovereignty of the states is an international one. The Ministry of the Interior has funds to subsidise arts festivals, the national theatres and operas, cultural activities in West Berlin and the international film festivals (Berlin, Oberhausen, Mannheim). Among these subsidies are annual prizes for the best German feature film, and production grants for 'cultural' short films *(Kultur– und Dokumentarfilme).* Until the early Sixties (when, for three years running, the prizes for the best feature film could not be awarded for lack of suitable entries), the political dimension of the subsidies was unmistakable; the Minister regularly honoured films with a distinct anti-communist and pro-NATO slant, usually stories dealing with Germany's divided state from something of a Cold War perspective. When challenged on this, a Ministry spokesman once tartly replied: 'These prizes are gifts. It is our right to choose to whom we want to present them.' However utopian it would be to think that such a policy might encourage better films or help the international standing of the German film industry, the Ministry of the Interior became an important source of finance for young film-makers when in 1961 it was decided to award grants for feature film projects and scripts. Significantly, the first articulated protest and counter-organisation emerged from the ranks of the state-subsidised makers of 'cultural' shorts.

4 The Oberhausen Group: the first generation of 'independents'

Of the 26 film-makers, writers and artists who signed the manifesto at the 1962 Oberhausen Festival, most had acquired film experience through short films either subsidised by the Ministry or commissioned by oil companies and the chemical industry. Some, like Kluge, Reitz, Schamoni, Senft, Spieker and Houwer, had won prizes at international festivals. What stung them into action was a justifiable sense of being neglected at home:

> The collapse of the commercial German film industry finally removes the economic basis for a mode of film-making whose attitude and practice we reject. With it, the new film has a chance to come to life. The success of German shorts at international festivals demonstrates that the future of the German cinema lies with those who have shown that they speak the international language of the cinema. This new cinema needs new forms of freedom: from the conventions and habits of the established industry, from intervention by commercial partners, and finally freedom from the tutelage of other vested interests. We have specific plans for the artistic, formal and economic realisation of this new German cinema. We are collectively prepared to take the economic risks. The old cinema is dead. We believe in the new.

Even if the intentions seem rather general, to publish them at this point was none the less a shrewd move. The advocates of the 'Young German Cinema' did not attempt to storm the industry that had left them out in the cold, but rather assumed its demise as a proven fact – a premature assumption, as it turned out. Instead, they put forward a programme which was a calculated *mélange* of 'professional' and 'ideological' demands, obviously addressed to the Minister of the Interior in his role as representative of the country's cultural interests abroad.

The truly innovative aspect of the manifesto was that so many film-makers were able to unite on a common platform, despite the diversity of artistic and filmic interests. As a group, their influence on government circles was considerable. Thanks to spokesmen like Alexander Kluge, who became and remains the leading film 'politician' of the independents, the Oberhausen group successfully lobbied members of the Bundestag, chairmen of commissions and ministerial secretaries. The most tangible result of the lobbying was the formation in 1965 of the *Kuratorium Junger Deutscher Film,* a key institution in the later development of the German cinema because it was explicitly charged with putting the proposals of the Oberhausen manifesto into practice. With direct government funding but a selection committee made up mostly of film journalists, the Kuratorium sponsored the first films of Kluge *(Abschied von Gestern),* Pohland *(Katz und Maus),* Fleischmann *(Jagdszenen aus Niederbayern)* and Herzog *(Lebenszeichen);* and sixteen other features were fully or more often partly financed between 1965 and 1968.

The starting capital amounted to 5,000,000 DM over three years, with an average of 300,000 DM per film. The idea was that of a pump-priming operation, in the form of interest-free loans to be paid back and reinvested in further productions. In fact, very little of the money returned to the Kuratorium. The contracts drawn up between the Kuratorium and the successful applicants recognised the director of the film as the author *(Autorenfilm)* and privileged his position. This encouraged and in a sense even obliged the director to be his own producer and to set up small production units, on the lines of the French *nouvelle vague* director, though it would be misleading to assume the same degree of aesthetic and personal coherence in the Oberhausen group as existed among the French directors emerging from *Cahiers du Cinéma*.

Twenty films in three years represented a sizeable percentage of the output of a country whose film industry was in permanent crisis and on the brink of collapse. Not surprisingly, the work of the Kuratorium was felt to be a threat, and representatives of the established film industry began to lobby parliament for a new form of tax-concession to boost production almost as soon as the Kuratorium was set up. After years of public debate and haggling between the Kuratorium lobby and the commercial lobby, the government in 1967 passed the already mentioned Film Subsidies Bill (FFG). The bill provided that 0.10 DM was to be levied on every cinema ticket sold in West Germany and West Berlin (*Filmgroschen,* totalling about 15,000,000 DM annually) and passed on to the Film Subsidies Board (*Filmförderungsanstalt,* or FFA) for allocation and distribution. Unlike the Kuratorium, the FFA was an official federal institution, and, as such, again only able to dispense economic aid and not discriminate qualitatively. Once the bill was passed, the Ministry ceased to fund the Kuratorium directly and merely recommended to the federal states that they support it with a total of 750,000 DM per annum, a drastic reduction in its operational scope compared with the original 5,000,000 DM over three years. This was all the more severe for the 'Young German Film', as the FFA was designed to help only those already established as producers. The Board automatically subsidised a producer whose film had grossed 500,000 DM or more during its first two years of release, up to an amount of 250,000 DM, or 50% of production cost. This amount could only be used for financing another film. In other words, the subsidy was intended as a quantitative production bonus, except that a film with a quality rating had to gross only 300,000 DM for its producer to be given a grant for his next project. This reinstated the economic and political significance of the FBW, whose role had shrunk with the gradual abolition of entertainment tax on films. Since cinemas were closing at the rate of one a day, and audiences were staying away by the million (a loss of 80 million spectators a year), independent productions had to aim for a quality rating and thus adjust themselves to the ideological criteria of the FBW if they hoped to qualify for subsidies from the FFA. In fact, of the hundred-odd films that had received production grants from the Board by 1972, no more than eight or ten could be said to belong to the 'Young German Cinema'.

The reasons for this are simple. One had to have made a film (the so-called *Referenzfilm*) before applying to the Board, since the bill did not initially provide for subsidies on scripts or script-outlines, as in the case of the Kuratorium. Once the reference film was made, it needed a distributor. Production was again at the mercy of the prevailing distribution system, which is not synonymous with an objective assessment of popularity. Were a distributor found, financial success still depended on the amount of publicity he was prepared to invest in. It would therefore be premature to conclude that the 'Young German Cinema' was a failure with the public, as some journalists pointed out with satisfaction. Alexander Kluge, for instance, maintains that, caught between the monopoly position of the distributors and the 'automatic' system of subsidies operated by the FFA, the 'young' cinema had no proper chance to prove itself.

Although presented as equitable to all parties, the Film Subsidies Bill evidently advantaged the established distributors' production arms. Even the first amendment of the bill (1971), empowering a special committee to award a further subsidy of up to 150,000 DM to films classified as 'good entertainment' and to give grants to directors who had won a prize at one of the international 'A'-festivals, did little to redeem the Board's function in the eyes of its opponents, who dubbed it a 'soap-opera cartel' *(Schnulzenkartell)*. As a counter-offensive against Oberhausen, the bill was effective in driving independent directors to look for better opportunities in TV, and it hastened the dissolution of the original Oberhausen group. Some of the original signatories were prepared to 'go commercial' by trying to produce within the system the kind of pot-boiler that would give them the production grant necessary for the realisation of more personal projects. This was the case with Peter Schamoni, Hans-Jürgen Pohland and Rob Houwer, who are now generally considered commercial directors and producers. Others such as Volker Schlöndorff and Johannes Schaaf occupy an in-between position: they are actively interested in production values, quality entertainment and the future of the 'industry'. Schaaf, for example, when asked what he thought was wrong with German films, replied: 'We always keep the entertainment value as low as possible, which is ridiculous; no other country in the world makes films that way. I believe German directors always disregard the public's need to be entertained. If you look at Brook's *A Midsummer Night's Dream* what strikes you is, on the one hand, the clear and exciting interpretation of the Shakespeare text, and, on the other, all the show-values, so that the production could easily be put in an entertainment slot on TV and everyone would be delighted. I think it is important that a film can be consumed on different levels.'

Schaaf gives a description of how the Subsidies Bill might ideally have worked, but the actual bill was not only detrimental to the Oberhausen activists, but also disastrous for the industry itself. While the availability of easy money for commercial producers made production shoot up virtually overnight (1966 – 96 films; 1968 – 107 films; 1969 – 121 films), it encouraged a pernicious policy of throwing subsidy quickies on to the market; these recouped their investment in the shortest possible time by catering to a porn clientele largely recruited from Germany's 2,000,000 immigrant workers *(Gastarbeiter)*, or by purveying infantile low-brow schoolboy comedies to emotional adolescents of all ages. The sex wave and the classroom comedies ruined the market for commercial producers, since each new series had a briefer span before it ran aground on the public's apathy. They permanently disaffected the more demanding cinema audiences, and led to the closure of cinemas not located in the larger conurbations. As with the guaranteed credits of the Fifties, a production boom was foisted on a shrinking market, with predictable results; for the sake of short-term profits, the industry was prepared to jeopardise its economic future by creating a volatile and occasional public, unpredictable in its demands and tastes. The situation was not helped by the fact (again paralleling the experience of the Fifties) that production was largely in the hands of distributors, who, via block-booking, were able to dictate programme policy to the cinemas. In extreme cases, a cinema owner had to take half a dozen German porn films in order to be able to show an international success like *Midnight Cowboy* or *Cabaret*, even if he knew that there was no demand among his regulars for sex films. The distributors' dumping practices virtually starved second-run cinemas out of existence.

5 The Second Wave: in the ghetto of culture

By 1970 it was obvious that the early successes of the Oberhausen initiative were backfiring. Apart from helping to create the Kuratorium, the group had been able to press for the foundation of two film schools (Berlin and Munich), and their sympathisers generated such further schemes as the setting up of a German Film Archive in Berlin, and a cinema (the Berlin 'Arsenal') that functioned as a cinémathèque. These are permanent achievements. And yet most of their moves were pushing the cinema in the direction of culture and education, while the Film Subsidies Bill was making it clear to everyone that real power was with those who controlled finance and distribution. The bill had given one part of a moribund industry a new lease of life, but it had destroyed that part of it (the outlets and distribution circuits) on which the independents had to rely if they were to reach an audience at all. New films by young directors simply did not get into the cinemas.

In the first years after Oberhausen, distributors who did not want to miss the bandwagon actually advanced distribution guarantees. But as soon as they realised the advantages of the bill for their own production companies, they lost interest in the young German film and its directors. At the same time, the general euphoria of being able to make films at last led the Oberhausen group to neglect distribution strategy; there was little evidence in the films themselves of a coherent aesthetic or social commitment that would have allowed a wider public to identify and recognise what the 'Young German Cinema' stood for and wanted to achieve. Opinion polls showed that spectators were 'irritated, annoyed', that the films made them feel 'intellectually inferior'; some even expressed 'anxiety' because of the 'disconnectedness', 'lack of story' or 'disagreeable associations'. However doubtful the value of such polls, they do show the relative backwardness and lack of cinematic culture among those still frequenting the cinema, and also that film-makers were out of touch with the conscious or unconscious needs of their potential audience.

Had the established film industry been in a genuine position of strength, the fact that by 1971 over 30 features had not found any form of distribution would have sounded the death-knell for an independent cinema along these lines. Alternatively, had the government intervened at all levels, especially that of distribution, then the German cinema might have had a cinematically literate public and also its own Chabrol or Truffaut (i.e., commercial directors who command a national and international audience). As it happened, the quantitative measures (the Subsidies Bill) led to crudely speculative exploitation of an already depleted market, and the qualitative changes (awards and project-grants from the Kuratorium and the Ministry of the Interior) isolated the film-makers and exposed them to the risks that Schaaf describes very graphically:

> If you only get subsidies, they are necessarily a temptation to either cheat or go bankrupt ... For what are the criteria of a selection committee when it picks a particular script for subsidy? Doubtless the criteria that the individual members have derived from, say, the films of Fellini, Rosi or Truffaut. But their films are made on considerably higher budgets. This means that you have to submit a script that meets these criteria but then it needs at least 6-800,000 DM to get made. Now, assuming our producer-director gets his grant of, say, 200,000, he then boldly approaches different distributors to raise the rest. But they don't give him an advance because they're sceptical about the project. Industry and banks don't do so either, they prefer to invest in tankers, or something that's tax-deductible. Our producer-director now sits on his cheque for 200,000 DM and can't do anything with it. He is in a fix, psychologically and financially. Psychologically, he wants to make his movie, express himself, communicate – otherwise it kills him. Financially, there's the cheque, which expires if it isn't used. To get out of this dilemma, he starts his 800,000 DM film on, say, 300,000, which means a shorter shooting schedule, he can't work with professionals but has to ask his friends, his actors are picked off the street. Of course he doesn't do this naively, but tries to make a virtue of necessity, so that it becomes a matter of style. Only he didn't plan his film that way, and a crucial discrepancy develops between his original conception and his economic possibilities. And this discrepancy is usually fatal. It's like trying to build a Rolls-Royce with money that's just enough to make a bicycle ... And so everything has to be done in the cutting room; that's where he can have a field day. And that's why these films are edited in such a complex way, all the art goes into the editing ... The aesthetic complexity of our 'social-criticism' films stands in no relation to their ideological content ... These films are so complex and abstract that nobody can follow what is going on ... I get the feeling that much of the political commitment in film-making is nothing but an attempt to charm committees who award grants and prizes.

Schaaf, who belongs to the Oberhausen generation and has two moderately successful films to his credit, is certainly somewhat cynical in his last point, but he puts his finger on a real dilemma: the subsidies and grants are (in the words of another film-maker) 'too little to live on and too much to die on'. They are awarded on the implicit assumption that what the film-maker produces is a crafted object like a painting or a sculpture, but for the director the illusion of artistic autonomy is immediately dispelled in the production phase, when the film appears as a commodity that needs to circulate in order to exist.

Unlike the commercial director or producer who orients his film towards a particular audience from the moment he thinks about a subject, the state-subsidised film-author has to protect his conception, his dream film, against the contingent (though real enough) market priorities and economic restraints. But unlike a painter, he cannot escape his social obligations; after all, he uses a lot of tax-payers' money to realise a private fantasy. So he has to woo a public he cannot even count on; his style becomes nothing more mysterious than an attempt to surmount the peculiar suspension that he feels, working in a social vacuum. The public's difficulties with many such films, on the other hand, spring from their ambivalent stance vis-à-vis the viewer: self-expression is either stylised into anarchic satire (which only works by having fun at the audience's expense), or sublimates itself into a critical statement about German society, and this kind of distance is invariably resented by a mass-audience as 'intellectual'. However disparate the best films of the new German cinema, it comes as no surprise to find in the films of Herzog, Syberberg, Schroeter and Wenders, for example, an unusual degree of aesthetic closure towards formal beauty and abstraction, a refusal to be explicit on the level of argument and meaning. Sensuousness, colour, and emotional luxuriance to the point of morbidity lure the viewer into accepting as valid discourse a social stance that is poignantly defensive and individualistic to a vulnerable extent. A style has evolved in the German cinema of the last five or six years that vacillates between satirical realism and symbolism of almost oppressive obliqueness, a style not unconnected with the cultural limbo affecting much of Germany's intellectual life today.

No director has assumed his 'displacement' as lucidly and ruthlessly as Werner Herzog, even in his choice of subject and locale (none of his films to date has a contemporary German setting, and his documentaries seek a characteristically extreme angle of approach). Since having his first feature financed by the Kuratorium and receiving a federal prize, Herzog has proceeded on an alternation of prizes and advances for scripts. Neither *Lebenszeichen* nor *Even Dwarfs Started Small, Fata Morgana* or *Aguirre* has ever had regular distribution in Germany. Not unreasonably, Herzog thinks his films will come into their own 'in the next fifty years' rather than now, and his attitude most closely approximates to that of an artist creating 'works' in a more traditional medium like literature or painting.

One often hears the complaint about state-subsidised film-makers that they live in a ghetto, much like the people working in state-subsidised theatre, opera and ballet. It is true that Germany's independent cinema is guaranteed mainly by the fact that the state is sufficiently affluent to play patron to its 'arts', not least because it can buy an appreciable amount of international prestige thereby, and at relatively small expense. The film-makers know as well as anyone how precarious and dependent their 'independence' is; Herzog, for instance, talks about being given 'artificial respiration'. When seeing films under the 'New German Cinema' banner, one can never wholly disregard the 'official' nature of their existence. It looks as if the German film industry's initial handicap – its home market orientation – is boomeranging, insofar as independent productions are now exported via embassies and cultural institutes without having a home market that would authenticate them as products of the social and cultural reality they are supposed to represent. In the context of international film criticism and festivals the political implications of their style are neutralised, the critical engagement that expresses itself through apparently esoteric material and hermetic forms can no longer be read as such, so that many of the films are ultimately as unsuitable for an international market as Germany's commercial productions, albeit for opposite reasons. Yet ironically, film-makers depend on their reputation abroad in order to continue receiving grants and prizes at home.

The paradox has made some of them attempt to opt out of their ghetto-existence. The passage through the bottleneck of distribution and the subsidies/open-market-finance deadlock is TV, which has become the patron saint of the new independent feature. What the Kuratorium was for the Oberhausen generation, the eight TV networks now are for the second wave: an indispensable source of finance, and a possibility for constructive work in a mass medium. Thanks to the particular structure of West German TV, with its regional bases all commissioning films and features for the two national channels and the more esoteric (regional) third channel, an independent film-maker can join the queue for freelance work. He can either sell his film to TV as a substitute for cinema distribution (he can even sell it several times to different regional stations), or he can offer the project to a network as a co-production in order to bridge the gap between a government grant and the required budget. If he is a known quantity, he may even have his film completely financed by TV: Herzog's *Aguirre, Wrath of God* was a TV-cinema co-production, while his short feature on the ski-jump champion Walter Steiner *(The Great Ecstasy of Woodcarver Steiner)* was wholly produced by SDR, the Southern German network. Most of Wim Wenders' films are TV co-productions, and so are Syberberg's.

There are, however, film-makers who reject on principle any participation in a secondary circuit of subsidised privilege, and who accept the withering away of the commercial cinema as a necessary consequence. From about 1968 onwards, a more radical conception of film-making became associated with the Berlin Academy of Film and TV. While the Munich film-school products are more typical of the tendencies described above (Wenders is their most promising graduate to date), Berlin students have gone back to the traditions of documentary work and film-journalism. They are de-industrialising the cinema even more than the independent productions of the producer-director-writer generation, which means that films are made only within a specific social or political context. The aim is to serve the informational and agitational needs of certain groups: strikers, miners, foreign workers, slum families, women's rights groups.

Important impulses for community-oriented film-making have emerged from this work, often in direct competition with current affairs programmes and documentary features put out by TV. Some films do this successfully, and quite a number of film-makers trained in Berlin are in fact working for TV, either permanently (Klaus Wildenhahn) or on a freelance basis (Farocki/Bitomsky, Ziewer/Wiese, Lüdke/Kratisch). A genre of 'workers' films' has found its way on to TV, with provocative titles like *Rote Fahnen sieht man besser* (1971) and *Liebe Mutter, mir geht es gut* (1972). *Die Wollands* (1972), *Lohn und Liebe* (1973) and *Familienglück* (1975) employ fictionalised situations and a recognisable plot to reach peak-time audiences, and it is in this context that Fassbinder's family series *Acht Stunden sind kein Tag (Eight Hours are not a Day)* belongs; it looks no less original for being not altogether unique.

The fact that the series aroused almost unanimous disapproval among left-wing film-makers and critics must be seen partly as a reaction against Fassbinder's versatility, the fact that he has a foot in every door. When one studies the background to his production, one discovers a careful pattern of TV co-productions, commissioned work, films produced by his own company, subsidised films, production grants and prizes. By negotiating all the different sources of finance, Fassbinder has compromised himself in the eyes of the left, but one cannot deny that he has maintained a delicate balance between authorial freedom with financial risks and financial security under TV production control.

Most film-makers who work with TV companies have less freedom than Fassbinder, and some of them feel they are in a cleft stick: the films they make with TV money have very little chance of reaching the cinemas, and yet they hanker after 'real' cinema audiences. Alternative distribution circuits are therefore more than ever promoted by the film-makers themselves; the most successful attempt in this area has been the founding of the Filmverlag der Autoren in 1971, as a company which acts as a self-distribution for the producer-directors. The Filmverlag distributes almost all the films of Fassbinder, Wenders, Hauff, Brandner and Kluge – about 50 films made by German directors during the last decade. With the Kuratorium now channelling some of its funds into promotion grants, the move towards revitalising the cinema circuits has gathered momentum. Small cinemas in the larger cities are being run by collectives or individuals for a more specialised audience that appreciates a carefully worked-out programme. This is a relatively novel idea in Germany, where going to the cinema still has a very low social prestige. If the Berlin 'Arsenal' has shown the way for a cinematically literate programme policy, an important precedent was set in Frankfurt, where a 'communal cinema' subsidised by the municipal council was taken to court by local cinemas but cleared of their charge of unfair competition. Subsequently, similar cinemas have appeared in other towns, and although by themselves these numerically insignificant outlets cannot support a German independent cinema, they give the directors some of the desired feedback from the public. Alexander Kluge, for example, often travels with his films, so that he can be challenged in discussions.

Kluge's example shows that after the high hopes of the early Sixties, when taking over the industry was the order of the day, independent film-makers have become more realistic and accepted the cultural field as their domain. While fully exploiting the various sources of finance and production which the system offers them (extended through amendments to the Subsidies Bill in 1974, when a certain number of TV co-productions each year and project-subsidies were guaranteed by law), many recognise an educational and political task. If it exists at all as a reality beyond the journalistic tag, the 'New German Cinema' is being built upon several fronts, from the grass roots upwards. At present, it functions as a secondary circuit, its only tenuous link with a mass public being TV. Regarded in the light of commercial viability, this is a weakness. It is a strength, however, when one considers the extraordinary breadth of possibilities which such a flexible deployment of talent and resources has actually produced.

Making an Impact – Rainer Werner Fassbinder and the Theatre

Peter Iden

The newspaper *Bremer Helfer* called it a 'Showdown', the programme through which Rainer Werner Fassbinder rose from a Munich basement theatre to the big stage of a civic theatre and into the public eye. It was a windy day at the beginning of November 1969: the theatre in Bremen was showing two Fassbinder films (*Katzelmacher* and *Love is Colder than Death*) and two of his pieces for the stage – his version of Goldoni's *Coffee Shop* and the cabaret-like revue *Anarchy in Bavaria*. Rarely has a talent emerged as forcefully as did Fassbinder's that day. Everything came over distractedly: the sputtering pacing and exaggerated artifice of the Goldoni adaptation, and Fassbinder himself in a discussion afterwards, scarcely capable of formulating anything, almost idiotically inarticulate. But it was also clear that here was a man to be reckoned with. The certainty felt at that time in Bremen has been brought into question with each of his new stage productions since. That's what makes it so difficult to establish a perspective on his work; in retrospect, the Bremen performances seem like a beginning whose indications haven't been followed up in subsequent developments. What did follow was a series of new beginnings. One had to reconcile oneself to the fact that there's no consistent principle in operation; no unified reflection on the theatre is definable in the work.

This 'Showdown', a hiatus in the career and work of an author-director (who was 23 when he came to Bremen), also marked a new start, a turning-point, for Kurt Hübner's Bremen Theatre. It was the penultimate one in a series; the final phase of Hübner's work in the town came when the designer Wilfried Minks graduated to directing. Hübner had discovered Fassbinder in the Munich *anti-teater* (he saw *The Threepenny Opera*). The working methods that Fassbinder had practised with a group of young actors in the basement theatre were still in evidence in the Bremen *Coffee Shop,* and remained a reason why the group's entry into the established theatre world – first in Bremen, then in Bochum – couldn't occur without conflicts. What distinguished Fassbinder and the group's methods? A great spontaneity in the playing, the tendency to explain the choice of material as arbitrary, random and irrational factors in the handling of the productions ... but also vehemently passionate acting, and a light, nonchalant kind of aggressiveness. Fassbinder's path in the German theatre has retained these characteristics, even though he has separated himself more and more from the group.

But isn't his path in the theatre just a sidetrack in his general growth to artistic maturity? An examination of all his post-Bremen activities reveals a clear bias towards film and TV. There have still been cross-currents between film and theatre, pieces like *The Bitter Tears of Petra von Kant* and *Bremen Freedom* which were done in both media. But the film projects greatly outnumber the theatre projects. However, one should conclude that Fassbinder's interest in film is stronger than his interest in theatre only with great caution. He invariably returns to the theatre – and is invariably repelled by the prevailing limitations (having eventually found them inhibiting and constricting in Bochum). And at the same time problems in the theatre haven't destroyed his concern for the implementation of a progressive theatre practice: because the possibility of controlling one's means and developing them further presents itself more readily on the stage than in the cinema. That is undoubtedly the main consideration behind the decision to take over the Frankfurt TAT [Theater am Turm] in the autumn of 1974.

What's striking in the mass of films is also evident in the theatre work to date: an overflowing talent, prolific to the point of self-injury, confused, but energetically switching material, style and aesthetic position. In the working notes for the adaptation of Lope de Vega's *The Burning Village,* one takes all the datelines – Munich, Madrid, Fuerteventura, Las Palmas and Paris – as tokens of the restless mobility of an author who is always somewhere other than (even if not necessarily any further than) his audience. And so, as far as Fassbinder's theatre work is concerned, one confronts an 'oeuvre' that refuses to be pinned down and defined as an entity, but rather presents itself as a series of disparate statements. Hasty, stark productions, often put together in minimal time under great pressure. Quixotic stories about plays and their performances, inadequate preparation and inconsequential realisation to match ... anyone who talks about Fassbinder and the theatre has to take these aspects into account too. There was some surprise hidden behind the announcement of each new project. Titles appeared on schedules when the plays themselves hadn't even been written (for example, *The Gentle Tangos of the Fascists* in the Frankfurt programme); adaptations were presented, and it seemed evident – as Fassbinder readily admitted – that the author had scarcely read the originals *(The Coffee Shop, The Burning Village).* Such disorientations haven't mitigated Fassbinder's appeal and success in the theatre – rather the opposite. It's a success founded on his steadfast need for expression, but also on the theatre audience's thirst for novelty in the late Sixties and early Seventies. And at the same time profiting from the shortage of playwrights, and the difficulties that other authors encountered in dealing with contemporary realities. Fassbinder opened plays in Bremen, Bochum, Nuremberg, Frankfurt and Berlin; always occasions of tense expectation, they were often followed by disappointment and groans of complaint. With the distinct exception of his *Bremen Freedom* (which was a 'real' play), Fassbinder has always made an impact in the theatre. He tossed them off, the evening of the performance making each provocation a thing of the past. It was his good luck that our theatre couldn't do without them. He used them boldly, and turned away from them immediately.

Since the individual qualities of these 'provocations' don't cohere into any kind of continuity, the only way one can characterise Fassbinder's theatre work is by sketching descriptions of a (necessarily partial, and arbitrary) selection of plays. The aim is not to post-rationalise the works' discontinuities into some grand design. Hence our choice of five examples: *The Coffee Shop* (Bremen, late 1969), *The Burning Village* (Bremen, late 1970), *Blood on the Cat's Collar* (Nuremberg, March 1971), *The Bitter Tears of Petra von Kant* (the Frankfurt 'Experimenta', June 1971), and *Bremen Freedom* (Bremen, December 1971). Work from a period of only three years. But the more recent productions, up to the staging of Ibsen's *Hedda Gabler* in Berlin early in 1974 (and taking into account what emerged from the *débâcle* with Peter Zadek in Bochum), don't go far enough beyond these five examples to eclipse them. Fassbinder himself wrote three of them *(Blood on the Cat's Collar, The Bitter Tears of Petra von Kant* and *Bremen Freedom)* and in the other two cases adapted an existing text *(The Coffee Shop, The Burning Village)*. He directed three of them himself *(The Coffee Shop, Blood on the Cat's Collar* and *Bremen Freedom)*, while Peer Raben did the other two *(Petra von Kant* and *The Burning Village)* under his guidance. Once, in *Blood on the Cat's Collar,* the author-director also appeared on stage as an actor. One incidental factor linking these productions is that former *anti-teater* players could be seen in them; Margit Carstensen, whom Fassbinder 'discovered' in the Bremer Ensemble, was also there from the start.

Five examples to illustrate one of the most productive talents that has come forward in the German theatre in the last few years, all bearing witness to Fassbinder's many-faceted abilities, but also to his many-faceted weaknesses. And so, a whistle-stop tour of a few initiatives:

1   The Coffee Shop [Kaffeehaus] or: Games from other Games
Fassbinder's adaptation of Goldoni's comedy (written in 1750) had one novel aspect that has recurred in his subsequent appropriations of material from other sources: the way that one reality displaces another, itself in turn compounded from elements of very disparate worth. Goldoni's play, in which one Don Marzio (a tiresome, parasitic gossip and informer) is eventually driven out of Venice, reveals the blackening of a character and the society that produced him through a number of intersecting, omnivorous emotional and financial transactions. Fassbinder amplifies the characters' social definition (the sole exception being the servant Trappolo, who becomes an interesting contrast-figure) and turns Don Marzio into a melancholy (almost Schnitzler-esque) figure, whose sadness and morbidity stand at the centre of the conception. Wilfried Minks' set for the production refers to Peter Stein's version of *Tasso* at the same theatre: this time there's a rosy carpet, a tall glass structure with a dummy cake on top, and on either side a male and female nude as erotic aperçus. All the actors are present in this space throughout, attractively costumed, moving between black chairs; despite the opulence, they're in bare feet and they have Colts on their hips. Venice and a Western saloon. Images as syntheses of images. The production is very slow, as if everything were drawn from some deep paralysis; the characters mingle, steal

past each other, lose themselves in little games – like adjusting their pose, making little sorties, conjuring a vague memory. Fassbinder quotes movements and poses from Stein's *Tasso,* compositions from his own films and those of Straub, and stances typical of Gary Cooper and Bruno Ganz. And in the female parts, Brigitte Janner and Margit Carstensen recall Jutta Lampe and Edith Clever.

If one considered that the mannerism of Stein's *Tasso* served to make the play 'transparent' in its context for those playing it, then the only element of that left here was the mannerism, without the critical perspective. This entire adaptation-cum-production was games from other games, performances from other performances.

2   The Burning Village [Das brennende Dorf] or: Revolt as an Obscene Gesture

This evening, too, disintegrates into noisy, contradictory moments (directed by Peer Raben). In Lope de Vega's original, King Ferdinand leaves the village Fuente Ovejuna in the hands of a high-ranking official. The latter is a cruel governor: when he abducts a girl who has refused him, shortly before her wedding, the villagers kill him. Ferdinand holds a tribunal, but can find no single culprit; the only answer he gets to his question 'Who killed the official?' is the name of the village itself. Impressed by the show of solidarity, he lets everyone go without punishment.

This appeasement, the apotheosis of the ruler's leniency, is altered in Fassbinder's version: Ferdinand hosts a feast for the village, at which he intends to hang all the farmers. What happens instead is that the accused men seize the king, the queen and their attendants from the throne, and eat them.

This last image of the blood-swilling horde has been anticipated earlier. The murder of the official (whom Fassbinder calls 'the commander'), mooted and carried out by the village women, turns into a bloodbath. The women overwhelm the man, bury him under their own bodies, tear him apart, and we seen them wallowing in his blood on the ground. The message: these rebels, who eat their oppressor, have become beasts ... were beasts all along. The girl Laurentia, who later lays into the official, intimates it in her very first scene: how she's cooked a dish that tastes like human flesh. Throughout the adaptation, there's a lot of similar evidence that Fassbinder sees the whole thing as being on a knife-edge between sex and power, instinct and ecstasy, revolt and mindlessness. The women laud the official's powerful cock. When they kill him, it's obviously not just an act of revolt against despotism and terror, but also – and much more strikingly – an enormous, collective orgasm. That is what is socially untenable about this adaptation: that it understands the farmers' liberation only as a release of their sexual instincts.

And so here again social references and motivations are broached through perverse forms, like those of frenzy or orgiastic mindlessness.

3   Blood on the Cat's Collar [Blud am Halsband der Katze] or: It's a Shame about People

After the adaptations, a play of Fassbinder's own. Phoebe Zeitgeist, the invariably nude title-character of the well-known American comic strip, who is forever submitting to horrendous tortures, moves through the play like a double of Ondra's daughter in Strindberg's *Dream Play*. She watches everything that the other characters do and say, and tries, as if she were from another planet, to find out which verbal and gestural conventions people use to communicate with each other. In the last third of the play she thinks she's grasped the way it works, and starts trying to return words and gestures to the players she learned them from. But having heard nothing but words and seen nothing but gestures, Phoebe can only repeat them parrot-fashion ... so that she may use a phrase conveying hatred when she wants to express affection. The strangers' learning process remains uncompleted; their reactions come back disoriented, mad. Their irritation at this miscomprehension finally leads them into a state of torpor; insofar as she demonstrates that forms of communication aren't working, Phoebe paralyses the vital nerve of her environment.

The play says that all we ever learn is the wrong thing; the world's woes are just that; all that we can do about them is moan. And so there's a lot of complaining. For Nuremberg, which had commissioned both the play and the production, the *anti-teater* actors (under Fassbinder's direction, he also appearing amongst them, sitting around lazily at an inn) turned on an agreeable casualness, a nice, soft imperturbability of expression. They moved as if they were going into a trance, pretty girls and various kinds of men in an endless round of puzzles. The scenes emitted a strange, seductive perfume, a suspicion of desire, of scorching along on heavy motorcycles, of curious adventures and weary depressions in their wake, of crime in the background, of small-talk at pimps' cocktail parties. Such small, vague attractions gave the production its value.

Fassbinder's attempt to deal with the unreliability of our conventions of social discourse belongs alongside plays by Gombrowicz and Handke. But *Blood* doesn't have the poetic strength of Gombrowicz, or the analytic coolness of Handke. Fassbinder's theatre here is static and lacking in perspective. Put forward as an image of sickness, but as a description of circumstances, not as a logical consequence.

4   The Bitter Tears of Petra von Kant *[Die bitteren Tränen der Petra von Kant]* or: Real Feeling

Fassbinder's work was written with the encouragement of the organisers of the fourth 'Experimenta' and produced in Darmstadt for the Frankfurt premiere by Peer Raben; it has since been filmed by the author himself. [A brief account of the film can be found in the documentation at the back of this volume.]

The stage version finds Fassbinder looking for yet another beginning. Its starting-point is a question: how much of the reality of a feeling (love, jealousy, hatred) can be expressed, and with which of the theatre's means? This stance clarifies the depiction of the glossy-magazine world of a sophisticated lesbian fashion designer (Fassbinder saw Carstensen in the role from the beginning) who is abandoned by her lover, as both a field of reference and a sustained reality. But the work then loses sight of its starting-point, in that it understands feeling exclusively in terms of exaggerated sentimentality, and shows it pathetically. On the other hand, all appearances to the contrary, it was Fassbinder's most earnest attempt to penetrate something other than a merely artistic reality.

5 Bremen Freedom [Bremer Freiheit] or: Live and Let Die

The Bitter Tears of Petra von Kant could be seen as an attempt to develop hackneyed, trivial material to such an extent that it begins to yield something that one often comes up against in Fassbinder's plays and adaptations: a trial of the credibility or otherwise of the pathetic, solitary figure on the stage. *Bremen Freedom,* whose first performances he produced himself in Bremen, extends this trial of the validity of strong emotions, weighty gestures and decisive actions, to the point where it enters its riskiest phase: in tragedy. The play draws on Bremen records of the last century about one 'pretty Gesina', a famous poisoner. The preparation of the source material has a literary-historical reference point in another play, written at about the time of the Gesina case: Hebbel's *Maria Magdalene*. As there for the girl Klara, so for Geesche Gottfried in *Bremer Freedom* the world is a place without freedom, a place of oppression under a rigid system of bourgeois values which allow a wife no life of her own. In both plays, fathers embody this system. Hebbel ultimately allows his Master Anton some inkling of the deadliness of the order that he himself stands for: he loses his grip on the world. Where Hebbel ends (on a note of doubt, questioning the old order), Fassbinder begins. His Geesche doesn't put up with her lack of freedom, but sets herself free stroke by stroke, death by death. 'And me?' are her first words in the Bremen production. They give fair warning: someone has been forced in on herself, is beginning to think about herself.

And beginning to do something for herself. The play's individual scenes are constructed by analogy. Soon enough, the very things that the wife suffers will be acted out; we will see those who are responsible die. The husband who bosses her around and humiliates her in front of friends; the children on whose account she decides not to marry someone else; the other man himself; later someone who endangers her enterprise; a cousin, a brother, and finally a girlfriend ... there's arsenic in the tea for each of them, and none of them outlives the scene in which he or she is introduced. But the elimination of constraints is never more than temporary; the oppressors keep coming back. When the creditor, demanding the return of borrowed money, meets his end, the brother, whose only interest in Geesche is in belittling her, is waiting in the wings. Finally the murderess is discovered. 'Now I'll die,' she says, and sings once again the pious song with which she has seen through every sacrifice.

So what's it about, this plot that plays Hebbel's bourgeois tragedy as a drama of liberation? The title *Bremen Freedom* is doubly cynical: freedom isn't what Geesche achieves, and freedom isn't what she seeks so murderously. It's possible here to detect a tendency that is critical of contemporary revolutionary praxis. Not only is Geesche's dependence out of all proportion socially, but 'false' too is the way that in pursuing her ideal of freedom she perverts it.

Fassbinder's production didn't go into this political aspect more specifically: it was more concerned with the working aesthetics of the stage than with the social dimensions of the material. Fassbinder, the actress Margit Carstensen (as Geesche) and the designer Minks were investigating the possibility of bringing together different levels of reality within the framework of a stage presentation. Minks furnished the symbolic level: at 'Concordia' (the Bremen studio theatre), a flat, dark cross constituted the playing area. It was surrounded by a mass of red plastic, on which individual pieces of furniture – the sideboard with the poison, a sofa, a dressing table – floated, as if on a sea (of blood?). Grey, Hitchcockian gulls were painted on the walls, and the audience rostra, decked out with portholes and the shapes of galleons, looked like ships. It was a wholly explicit image: the cross stood for the old order, which was all 'at sea'.

As far as acting style was concerned, Fassbinder and Carstensen decided on a formal transition from a cold realism to mannered, devious gestures, through which feelings of love, desire and suffering (not to mention a buzzing, anarchic glee after every murder) were expressed.

End of the tour. What conclusions can be drawn? Fassbinder's path in the theatre as a director and in drama as an author has always been a journey through the old materials and forms of the medium (the same is true of his film work). A journey, but also an obstacle course: sometimes it seems as if Fassbinder's work gets as much of its impetus from enthusiasm for things already discovered and thought out as from the impulse to demolish them in order to create anew according to his own ideas in the context of the old. The examples cited above bear witness to his efforts to define himself alone and through others. His own appearances in the plays pose the same problems. They rest upon the (theatrically vital) mediation of the historical context. Realities, bygone and current, are rearranged, artistic quasi-realities are substituted. It has often been thrilling to witness these substitutions. But both the adaptations and the productions have also suggested a great loss of reality. If Fassbinder wants to intensify his theatre work in Frankfurt, he'll have to settle down to something that he's always hitherto avoided: he has to perceive reality and, facing up to it, hold his own ground. If that happened, the diffuseness of his stage productions to date would simply become a feature of a prelude.

Translated by Tony Rayns

A Cinema of Vicious Circles

Thomas Elsaesser

Do you want to make German Hollywood films?
Yes. I'm all for it. Yes, that's what I want.
... I believe that all feelings are potentially exploitable, and are actually being exploited.

Like many other directors of his generation, Rainer Werner Fassbinder has had to rely at times on State prizes and project subsidies. Even though his first feature was financed by a private patroness, his film-making career (as opposed to his rise in the theatre world) only got under way after his second, *Katzelmacher,* gave him a handsome working capital: it cost about 80,000 DM to make, and received a total of 650,000 DM in prizes. (Another 300,000 DM came from the Film Subsidies Board two years later.) Under the circumstances, it mattered little that the film was a commercial failure. To Fassbinder himself, however, it did matter. For at a time when quite a few film-makers began to resign themselves to the fact that the new German cinema was producing consumer goods for a luxury market of art cinemas and third-programme TV, Fassbinder began to work at a different approach.

A commercial career

The following is a somewhat speculative attempt to indicate a possible logic in Fassbinder's cinema and its evolution, not in terms of a stylistic history developing its own momentum, but more in the light of his own stated intentions as they emerge in the interview extract quoted above. For him, being a 'German Hollywood' director implies being popular, commercially successful, and at the same time not uncritical of the society which his films reflect. Measuring the success or failure of this ambition in box-office or any other purely quantitative terms is impossible: figures are almost impossible to come by, while the system of State subsidies and the difference between cinema and TV showings (not to mention the vagaries of the German and international distribution circuits) all seriously distort the picture. None the less, what one can say is that after more than 25 films in six years, Fassbinder is still far from possessing a solid economic independence as a producer, even though he is the best-known and possibly the most popular film-maker in West Germany since the war.

In search of an audience

The question about his popularity may have to be phrased differently: given an ambition to be popular, what strategy can or must a film-maker evolve in order to make contact with an audience or with different kinds of audiences? In other words, what audiences are, in fact, 'written into his films'?

Fassbinder exemplifies the director-producer who is determined to be a commercial film-maker at a time and in a country where no viable commercial cinema exists, and where no ideologically unified basis for a popular cinema can be assumed. The class differences and antagonisms (especially those that separate the working class from the petty-bourgeoisie or the radical intelligentsia) do not neatly divide between TV audiences and cinema audiences; Fassbinder is addressing with one and the same cultural product social groups who do not necessarily possess or recognise a similarity of interests. The discontinuities of his style and the repetition of his central motifs seem to have sprung from this dilemma.

Fassbinder admits at least two distinct periods in his film-making: the films produced during his time with the Munich *anti-teater* (1969-70), including *Pioneers in Ingolstadt*; and the subsequent ones, starting with *Beware of a Holy Whore*, which was made a few months before *Pioneers*. In his own view, the main difference is that the first films were exercises in self-gratification, whereas the later ones were conceived with a particular audience-orientation in mind. 'By the time I made *Beware of a Holy Whore* I had found a way of using autobiographical material less onanistically, so that what I had to say about myself became more generally valid. I started to see myself in relation to the world around me, and that's the decisive difference between the *anti-teater* films and the later ones.'

Emotional exploitation

At no point during his career has Fassbinder renounced the autobiographical element in his films. His self-criticism does not affect the material but rather the manner of its presentation. The central experience – one might go so far as to call it the trauma that motivates his productivity – is emotional exploitation. His films are fictionalised, dramatised, occasionally didactic versions of what it means to live within power structures and dependencies that are all but completely internalised, and as such apparently removed from any possibility of change or development.

Repetition, reiteration therefore has a particularly important function in his work, on the thematic as well as the formal level. The films reproduce human relations 'as they are', while constantly retracing the contours of a circularity in the utopian hope of finding a way out at the weakest point. Much of the feel and impact of his films – an almost unbearably self-lacerating pessimism shot through with moments of ecstatic (and in the event gratuitous) optimism – seems to come from the need to discover a linearity or dialectic inside a situation emotionally experienced as inescapable, closed, self-perpetuating. Whether the roots of this trauma necessarily have to be sought in Fassbinder's private life is immaterial. As far as the films are concerned, they attempt to prove, with varying degrees of conviction, that the personal predicament has a wider symptomatic significance. And if Fassbinder's cinema shows any kind of progression in this respect, it is not in the way that his characters perceive escapes from the sado-masochistic bind, but in the remarkable inventiveness he shows, his concrete penetration of a contemporary social reality when orchestrating the theme across different human situations.

Thus *Katzelmacher* uncovers a vicious circle in the sphere of working-class relations to *Gastarbeiter,* where those kicked by the rest of society find others even more dispossessed than themselves, whom they exploit. A similar law governs sexual dependencies of whatever form (heterosexual in *Gods of the Plague,* lesbian in *The Bitter Tears of Petra von Kant,* male homosexual in *Fox*). With depressing inevitability, emotional exploitation also dominates and shapes the marital and family problems he depicts *(The Merchant of Four Seasons, Why Does Herr R Run Amok?, Wildwechsel, Martha,* etc.), the contacts and conflicts between races and classes *(Whity, Fear Eats the Soul).* It reappears at the place of work *(Eight Hours are not a Day)* and most recently in left-wing politics *(Mother Küsters' Trip to Heaven).*

Psychology or politics?

The economic and financial basis of this exploitation is never disguised, nor are the class conflicts anything other than just that: the demagogical side of the 'social partnership' propagated in West Germany is made apparent in concise scenes of Brechtian logic, such as those at the printer's in *Fox*. But insofar as Fassbinder, a socially and economically privileged member of society, discovers his own problems everywhere around him, he necessarily gives (much criticised) priority to the depiction of emotional dilemmas. The psychological dimension tends to usurp political economy, and it actually produces a reversal of roles, where emotional blackmail is seen to cut across classes (e.g., Hanna Schygulla's role as the model Karin in *Petra von Kant*). When a film attempts to run the two levels along parallel lines (as in *Fox,* the story of a proletarian hero who is sexually exploited and economically ruined by his bourgeois lover, as well as made fun of for his lack of education, his peasant manners and his naive admiration for middle-class values), it is the dramaturgy that suffers: from over-emphasis, redundancy and duplication. In *Fox,* the political analysis is contradicted by a lack of plausibility and verisimilitude. Predictably, the conflicts degenerate into a stark opposition of hero and villains, a less typical dramatic strategy in Fassbinder's work than is usually assumed.

The Hollywood model

Against the thematic continuity stands a not always linear development in Fassbinder's formal concept. This revolves round the film-maker's rapport with his audience. But if Fassbinder himself sees the main discontinuity in his work here, the break is in one respect perhaps less radical. His first film already shows an unmistakable stylistic gesture towards the aesthetic demands of commercial film-making: 'Right from the start we tried to go about film-making as if we were making real films. Even at a time when we couldn't yet get it right, and we didn't have the means, we always assumed that everything was already there, the experience and the finance.'

The crucial word here is 'real': at this stage it is somewhat naively understood as a reproduction of the Hollywood model. Like Godard, Melville and others, Fassbinder started out by imitating American movies, in particular gangster films *(Love is Colder than Death, Gods of the Plague, The American Soldier)*. As with Godard ten years earlier, imitation is scarcely the right word. What intervenes in both cases is an unhappy consciousness, a mixture of love of cinema and an acute sense of a historical position very different from the Hollywood of the Forties and Fifties, and an equally problematic discrepancy between movie-buff and movie-maker. None the less, the epigones of Hollywood in both France and Germany seem to have found the egocentricity of the outsider, the slightly self-pitying pessimism, and the latent misogyny of the *film noir* a common reference point for a tortuous discourse about a world of false images and real emotions, of public failures and private fantasies.

A form of revolt

But there the similarities end: if any of Godard's films has had a lasting influence on Fassbinder, it is not one of the 'American' films *(Bande à part, Le Mépris, Pierrot le fou)* but *Vivre sa vie*, with its theme of exploitation and prostitution in a morally and emotionally inarticulate milieu of social outcasts. Fassbinder has not followed Godard's political and intellectual dissociation from Hollywood. On the contrary, concentrating on one aspect of the Hollywood heritage (the production of 'real' feelings through 'false' images), he is attempting to reinvent Hollywood in the Germany of the Seventies. No doubt this is a complex phenomenon (the reception of the Hollywood cinema in West Germany is noticeably different from that in France, and dephased by a decade if not two), but certain elements stick out. As with France or Britain, the economic predominance of American films since the war has established Hollywood as the natural paradigm of picture-making. Furthermore, and this is perhaps especially significant in Fassbinder's case, Hollywood has been the horizon on which working-class youths and the occasional middle-class boy alienated from his own background grew accustomed to projecting their frustrated desires. Insofar as this cinema was outlawed by parental authority and ignored by the critical establishment until well into the Sixties, their enthusiasm articulated a temporary revolt. Thus the Hollywood idiom is the language that a German film-maker in the Seventies still shares with his predominantly under-30 working-class and lower-middle-class audience. What at first might have been the reflex of Fassbinder the movie-addict and would have exhausted itself in pastiche and parody, very soon became part of a conscious strategy for the director with commercial ambitions: to find and master a possibly degraded but none the less real form of communication with the actual or potential spectators of a popular cinema.

Pathos and inwardness

From the many emotional 'languages' that the commercial cinema has evolved, Fassbinder makes virtually no use of suspense, comedy or horror. His films have been described as sentimental, mawkish, moving between pathos and bathos, and it is true that he seems to concentrate rather exclusively on the varieties of pathos, understood as the emotional rhetoric of bourgeois tragedy and melodrama. The forms that this pathos takes, strident, with ironic overtones, or low-key, as in *Effi Briest,* might tempt one to think of it as personal, a kind of direct translation of what Fassbinder 'feels' about the world. On the other hand, it might well be a matter of translating his chosen theme: what romantic or domestic melodrama connotes in an unambiguous way is the presence of subjectivity in the discourse, a necessary precondition for an audience to feel affected by the victimisation in his films. However, the general basis on which this communication takes place – a certain diffuse emotionality, a mixture of nostalgia and regret, of operatic sentimentality and a somewhat cloying intensity – is not peculiar to Fassbinder. Here, he is in tune with many of his generation who have moved from a discovery of politics to a post-1968 inwardness. The hermeticism of a Werner Schroeter or the intellectuality of a Wim Wenders are middle-class versions of the same desire to codify a retreat. Except that in Fassbinder's work, because he explores the popular, low-brow dimensions of subjectivity, this retreat is also an advance, insofar as it discovers the realm of inwardness in members of a class who, except for a brief period in the Twenties, have always been excluded from it in German culture. What is problematic is that Fassbinder's populism may be the worst sort of compromise, aiming at a kind of embourgeoisement where everyone is allowed the luxury of self-pity.

But to return to Fassbinder's chosen path: the problem as it emerges from the films, is how to articulate threatening and aggressive emotional states (moments of betrayal, deception, manipulation, emotional cruelty, but also equally 'aggressive' manifestations of unconditional love, self-sacrifice, exuberance) in aesthetic forms that make them tolerated, acceptable. Fassbinder has ventured out into regions of extremes, where the directness of the emotional assault has to be mediated, and the spectator's susceptibility managed, channelled via the mechanics of identification and distanciation.

An emotional Verfremdungseffekt?

In the early films the problem is solved in a rather derivative manner: the stylisation of decor and effect oscillates between inadequacy (the physical and verbal gestures of the protagonists are never allowed to match their intentions) and over-elaboration (a mode somewhere between parody, primitivism and unintentional humour). In *Gods of the Plague* and *Pioneers in Ingolstadt,* for instance, the spectator is invited to identify with the characters, but also to laugh at them, to recognise the psychological situations and social conflicts, but also to be disturbed by their theatricality. None of the customary attitudes (whether comic distance or dramatic involvement) sits comfortably on these films. This unsettling, dephasing element has been interpreted as Fassbinder's Brechtianism, a sort of emotional V-effect. This may indeed be the case, although it seems equally possible that the particular form of distanciation and stylisation in the early films points towards the unresolved dilemma hinted at above – the troubled relationship of the would-be commercial film-maker to his one-time addiction as spectator-consumer. For it almost appears as if the self-alienation of the compulsive cinemagoer, his resigned and yet always revived voyeurism, is somehow taken into the films as the sad sediment of futility which spreads over the beautifully executed camera movements, the classically balanced shots, the languid pans.

Fassbinder is right; there is something masturbatory about these films, even if the shoddiness of the decor and the tinsel glamour of the actresses manages to moralise the attitude of self-satisfaction into a critical stance. Not only is the recurring topos of inadequacy the explicit sign of that ambition to make a 'real' Hollywood movie, of which the film one is watching is the touching, pathetic, melancholy echo, but the discontinuity which inadequacy implies also places the king-size dreams of the characters – defiantly asserted against an unresponsive environment – as ambitions fated with ludicrous inevitability to fizzle out ignominiously. The films thus reflect a twofold frustration: an imagination at second-hand is further foiled at the level of performance, and Fassbinder shows himself a realist with critical intentions only insofar as these are documents, records of what one might call emotional starvation fantasies. For this reason, perhaps, no unified emotional perspective was either possible or desirable.

Between awkwardness and beauty

The language, then, that Fassbinder shares with his audience in the early films is not the classical idiom of the affirmative Hollywood discourse (action, spectacle, strong effects), but this idiom curiously decentred by the gaping sense of emptiness that awaits the spectator afterwards, out in the street. The dialectics of escapism and realism, deeply embedded in the fabric of the American action film, are pulled apart by Fassbinder's gangster films. Voyeuristic projection is allowed to float dangerously out of its unconscious self-evidence (where an autonomous fictional spectacle normally keeps such impulses fixated), and emerges disjointedly as the unpleasant perception of the film as an artefact, or the exaggerated gesture of self-conscious make-believe: we begin to worry whether the actors themselves can keep up the pretence. This discrepancy, forced to the point of physical discomfort in films like *The American Soldier* and *Whity,* a discrepancy between awkwardness and beauty, lends itself to an ambiguous dialogue about the cinema itself, its manipulative images and its rhetoric of effect. But it also represents a provisional formulation of Fassbinder's moral theme, for he everywhere makes palpable – whether deliberately or by default – the sometimes terrifying and often grotesque distance between the subjective *mise en scène* of the characters and the objective *mise en scène* of the camera, between the way the characters perceive themselves, and the way that others (notably the viewer) perceive them. Thus pretensions that might have been expected to disavow themselves by their own lack of verisimilitude are none the less shown to exert a fascination over others, to the extent that they can be cashed in for power that causes real harm and hurt: Ricky, in *The American Soldier,* is an impossible Vietnam veteran turned hired killer. But given that the characters in this film are devoid of gestures or a language to call their own and gladly accept the simple coherence of the world of a gangster film, their willingness to act even the parts of the victims becomes much less implausible. What registers is the absurd but moving idealism that tries to live up to the exalted existence of small-time crooks and supermarket thieves. The films are as compulsive as watching a bad comedian, or the efforts of an assembly-line worker to keep pace with his machine.

Fassbinder's humanism

What is ambiguous and at the same time attractive about Fassbinder's early protagonists is that the degradation of their imaginative-emotional language (their imitations of tough guy or femme fatale mannerisms) and the degradation of their moral and social environment (they are failures, marginals, 'small fry') seem to cancel each other out, to create a precarious, momentary dignity: the typical commitment of Fassbinder's humanism. Whether the double argument about Hollywood glamour and the emotional grand guignol of the socially deprived amounts to a critique of either Hollywood or German society is another matter. Where it is effective is in reflecting the broken and unresolved relationship that an intellectual entertains with the proletarian residue, the unashamed sentimentality, the liberatingly vulgar and direct eroticism of a certain popular culture coming mainly from America.

From gangster movies to melodrama

The more Fassbinder became confident of his abilities, the more securely he could handle the authentic reproduction of inauthentic roles, the more the gangster film must have seemed to lead to an impasse. Such an essentially intellectual construction with its irritating but also amusing amalgam of bad faith and bad grace would not persuade a mass audience of prejudice-ridden, frustrated, disgruntled German petty bourgeois to abandon their TV talk shows and *Pornofilme.* A glance at Fassbinder's filmography from *The Merchant of Four Seasons* onwards shows him almost bending over backwards to meet his prospective audience halfway, by systematically experimenting with topical subject-matter, while focussing even more single-mindedly on the genre-formulation of a 'purer' form of melodrama. The strength of the tradition he adopted (the 'women's picture' of the Forties and Fifties) is that it dramatises what could be called processes of victimisation and negative emotional experiences in a realistic setting. What Fassbinder had to do was overcome the throwaway irony of his theatrical imitations of Hollywood (*Katzelmacher* and *Why Does Herr R Run Amok?* had already indicated the way) in order to discover a new naivety of cinematic expression, a nuanced, 'classical' way of representing strong emotions directly.

Here, the Hollywood masters could still teach him something: 'I would not be able to tell a film like *Marnie* simply the way Hitchcock does it, because I haven't got the courage of his naivety, simply to tell a story like this and then at the end give the audience this thing, this explanation . . . I wouldn't have the guts, because it also takes guts . . . maybe one day I'll have that courage myself, and then I'll be like Hollywood.' It is evident that Fassbinder since *Merchant* has moved from an essentially self-conscious form of distanciation (where the vulnerability of the pure and simple emotions that motivate his characters is disguised by overcompensated anti-stances: not just the tough guy and the vamp, but also the theatrical, tawdry atmosphere of petty vice, morbidity, exhibitionism and languid decadence) to a more straightfaced psychological and emotional realism. Instrumental in this change was, as is well documented, his discovery of the films of Douglas Sirk.

A solidarity of victims
If *Merchant* can be called Fassbinder's first film with a definite audience-orientation, it is less the realism of the setting or the ordinariness of the characters that measures it than the fact that the states of feeling are registered along a single dramatic and stylistic continuum: on the razor's edge, maybe, between risibility and tragedy, camp and kitsch, but what has disappeared is the ambivalence surrounding the characters' own role-playing, and with it the uneasy awareness of watching a documentary about people playing out a fiction. Fassbinder himself sees it as a question of what attitude the director assumes towards his characters. 'Would it be right to say that this attitude is characterised by the fact that the director does not put himself on a higher plane than that of his characters?' – 'Right' – 'That he doesn't comment on them, but understands them, views them on their own levels?' – 'That in the final instance he is one of them. That he admits to himself, in most respects he is like them, yes.' – 'Which doesn't exclude criticising them, although in this case criticism and self-criticism would fall together?' – 'Right.' – 'The film is therefore not conceived from a point of view outside . . . ' – ' . . . but from within . . . ' – ' . . . by means of presenting the contradictions inherent in the characters themselves?' – 'Yes, a dialectical process, if you like.' What Fassbinder and his sympathetic interviewer here formulate together is the principle of a 'liberal' *mise en scène,* as practised by the American directors of the Fifties (Sirk, Ray, Preminger, Minnelli, Losey): every character is justified within his own terms, there are no outright villains, only victims.

The typical situation in a Fassbinder film, where a mother/father, wife/husband or friend/colleague make demands on the hero/heroine that are sadistic, or betray, deceive or abandon him/her is dramatised in such a way that these dominating figures, from whom there is objectively or subjectively no escape, also have their reasons, are sometimes well-meaning or possess complex motives over not all of which they have control (cf *Merchant of Four Seasons, Wildwechsel, Fear Eats the Soul, Martha, Fear of Fear*). The hero, by contrast, is given a moral/emotional innocence that almost makes him the holy fool in a Dostoievskian world of universal prostitution. His simple-mindedness, his obstinacy in hanging on to simple truths and direct feelings become a form of higher wisdom, the gesture that unmasks the stupidity of self-interest, prejudice and oppression. Evil then appears depersonalised, as somehow inherent in the social system as a whole. What the films ultimately appeal to is solidarity between victims.

That this liberalism is problematic is known to Fassbinder himself. 'I think I'm one of the few directors in Germany who has a positive relation to his characters . . . in some cases, like the girl's father in *Wildwechsel* when he talks about the war, I'm indulgent almost to the point of irresponsibility.' In this remark are both the strengths and limits of the melodrama as a form of popular and critical cinema. Fassbinder's melodramas can and do make the very important distinctions between the different levels of individual motivation, between private morality and class morality, between human impulses and ideological impulses. It is by these disjunctions and discontinuities that Fassbinder develops his pathos, and through it he creates the vacuum in which social and psychological pressures become visible as they distort natural instincts and needs into manifestations of evil. But insofar as these pressures and forces cannot be named or analysed other than by pointing to their absence from the characters' consciousness, the purely inter-personal drama tends to imply that to understand is to forgive. Pathos becomes less a call to righteous anger ('I wanted to make them angry, as angry as I was, the people who watch action movies') than a sophisticated aesthetic effect that confirms inevitability.

The liberalism of being level with the characters and level with the audience ('What I aim at is an open realism . . . that doesn't provoke people into defensiveness') may be necessary to woo the spectator into giving himself over to the spectacle and thus opening himself emotionally via recognition and identification. But some of the recent films (notably *Fox* and *Mother Küsters' Trip to Heaven*) seem to indicate that Fassbinder himself is having doubts: they show an even more definite parti-pris for the hero/heroine, and they are less scrupulous about balancing the other characters' points of view. The spectrum of identification becomes narrower, and with it perhaps more radical. The villains are more like villains, their portrayal is elliptical to the point of parody. For that reason, these films are less convincing aesthetically, even though the director's point of view becomes clearer. That a certain moral ambiguity should be directly proportional to aesthetic persuasiveness seems to suggest that the path between making committed, critical cinema and being 'popular' within a basically bourgeois art form is a narrow one. Perhaps it is even a false alternative. For Fassbinder, the critical impact can only be transmitted indirectly ('the viewer should be able to activate things and feelings in himself via the characters, but the structure of the presentation ought to give him the possibility for reflection . . . that is, the *mise en scène* ought to be such that it makes distance and reflection possible'), and this is the main reason that he rejects distanciation through either satire or parody: 'I'm against caricatures, I'm against parodies . . . if you say that this scene [in *The American Soldier*, when the chambermaid commits suicide] has the effect of a parody, then I have to take your word for it, but then I'm ashamed of myself and I apologise.'

It is the psychological problem of how to keep in touch with the viewer's emotions that also determines his idea of realism: 'The only kind of realism that interests me is that which happens in the head of the spectators, not the realism on the screen.' This is why a more directly political analysis is rejected ('I'm not interested in making films that play with models or juggle ideologies') in favour of an overtly fictional realism which encompasses unrealistic, stylised, fairy-tale elements. 'I could imagine that the unrealistic elements in my films might bring the spectators closer to their own reality, and beyond, to a utopia. I don't believe that as a TV viewer theories are important to me, only as a reader of books. For a TV or cinema audience it's simply more important that those things are activated within me that also activate dreams and the like.' Fassbinder's notion of realism is thus remarkable not least for its frank admission of the habitual functions of escapist entertainment: encouraging daydreams, private fantasies, wish fulfilment ... except that he talks about liberation and utopia rather than escape.

More important than whether the films actually permit an audience to dream their own better future is that Fassbinder, in his search for an unprovocative realism that makes audience identification possible, has discovered for the German cinema the importance of being artificial in order to appear realistic. Both in decor and in language (the latter a condensed and as if foreshortened high-German that manages to be at once solemn and idiomatic), the effects are calculated to support and amplify the characters and their emotions. But by this very fact the realistic locations have something strangely symbolic. Against an atmosphere of 'naturalised' artifice, Fassbinder's Germany is more historically present than in many a political documentary.

A German setting for a German audience

Consequently, the melodramatic situations, the emotional anguish, the victimisation and isolation are shown to occur not only in a specifically German urban environment, but in the 'real' world – the place of work, the family, the block of flats with petty neighbours and tyrannical landlords, the supermarket and the launderette, the corner café and the local pub. Where the 'young' German film of the Sixties produced at best a flat, black-and-white naturalism, Fassbinder's carefully composed colour schemes, his selection of the typical detail available for an unobtrusive symbolism without being pressed into it, represent the kind of heightened realism that makes the traditionally closed world of the melodrama take on topicality, even where it wants to be existentially timeless.

As the direct memories and quotations of Hollywood fade from Fassbinder's cinema, the public written into the films becomes more definably German, ranging from working-class/petty bourgeois to petty bourgeois/intellectual. An audience, therefore, whose sensibility has been shaped by the *Wirtschaftswunder,* the ideology of self-discipline and self-exertion, and who are now (especially since '68) showing signs of being tired of more self-sacrifice and emotional frustration in the name of prosperity and political stability. That this class largely shuns direct political awareness by casting itself as the pitiful victims of overwhelmingly impersonal forces is a historical lesson that Brecht drew in *Mother Courage*. Fassbinder seems to accept this limitation, or rather it is the price he has to pay for his liberalism 'to the point of irresponsibility'; it may define for him the strategic point at which it is more important for an independent director to be 'popular' in a mass medium (which even Brecht's theatre never was) than to be politically explicit.

Recognition by repetition

In this sense, he has appropriated for himself other mechanisms of recognition that the mass media have perfected. They are present in his work on several levels. For instance, like Bergman since the Fifties, Antonioni and Godard in the early Sixties and Chabrol since the late Sixties, he has worked on creating his own 'series', externally identified by an actress, built up as a star and recurring from film to film (cf, Monica Vitti, Liv Ullmann, Stéphane Audran, Anna Karina . . . often the director's wife), made coherent by a central problem or constellation, of which the individual films are variations and amplifications. In Fassbinder's case, we have the films with Hanna Schygulla, the 'feminist emancipation' films with Margit Carstensen *(Petra von Kant, Martha, Fear of Fear)*, and the family melodramas with Brigitte Mira *(Fear Eats the Soul, Mother Küsters' Trip to Heaven)*. What this tendency among European directors reflects is the forces that come into play in a cinematic practice that is neither genre- nor studio-bound: a discrete, autonomous work in the bourgeois literary tradition is clearly inadequate, a single film not supported by a genre or series is too ephemeral and slight to create the kind of resonance necessary to establish a theme or a social setting 'realistically'. However, the very criterion of realism in the cinema seems to be closer to Jakobson's definition (that it is the cumulative effect of repetition and variation within a circumscribed pattern) than to Lukacsian notions of totality and representativeness. Among German directors, Fassbinder alone has created this resonance; his films impose themselves as just such a system of repetitions and variations.

But the fact that one can see the gradual emergence of a typical 'Fassbinder world' and its progressive consolidation (i.e. Fassbinder's growing interest as an 'auteur') points even more clearly to the material basis of his work: the existence of a team of virtually permanent collaborators (the equivalent of a mini-studio system) and the relative stability of his cast (a pocket version of the star system). At the same time, Fassbinder consciously uses what reputation he possesses, his status and personal charisma, for the realisation of his films. That he is the most publicised, interviewed, written-about director of the new German cinema obviously has something to do with his prolificness and the fact that he is equally at home in the cinema, TV and theatre, but it is perhaps also part of a strategy to extend the range of recognition (in the psychological sense) beyond the work to the author himself, conferring on his films an *a priori* aura of associations. Not since Brecht in the Twenties has a serious artist played with, exploited (the right word might be 'sensitised') the media with comparable success, in order to get access to the distribution apparatus and by extension the market. Even adverse comment is publicity, and the various skirmishes with the press or left-wing militants are so much grist to the mill. In 1973 when a reputable newspaper wrote him off as the 'tired boy wonder', the 'burnt-out genius' who was 'ruined by too much success too soon', he went on to outlive his obituaries by producing in the same year his two most successful films *(Fear Eats the Soul, Effi Briest).*

The pressure to produce

The point is perhaps that he can hardly do otherwise. Fassbinder's furious rate of production is at least in part a reaction against the constraints which the precarious financial circumstances of independent film-making force upon him. As such, the pressure to produce seems at times a flight forward. Because he is known to work very fast, he is never short of offers for co-productions from TV companies. His marketable asset there rests on his proven ability to bring in a film under schedule and below budget. The reason for this high degree of efficiency is the confidence he has gained from producing more than 25 films, putting him way ahead of other independent directors or freelance TV producers. Being in full employment all the year round in turn means that he can keep a comparatively large stock company at his own exclusive disposal. What would otherwise be a ruinous extravagance is thus a calculated risk. 'If I make a feature film where there are no salaries paid, the people working for me know with absolute certainty that next month, for another story of mine, there will be money. Maybe another reason is that because the films are made so fast they think to themselves "Either I hang around in Munich for three days doing nothing or I play a part that'll be seen by a lot of people who might offer me a job ... in that case, I might as well go there and stand in front of his camera." Of course, if I was making a film only once every three years and was still counting on people's idealism, that would be exploiting them.'

For better or worse, Fassbinder seems condemned to over-produce in order to produce at all, and in this sense he is the only independent film-maker in Germany whose working methods reflect the objective conditions of a capitalist mode of production, albeit in a pre-monopolistic, competitive phase. As such, he may well be anachronistic, a product of the curiously under-developed state of the German film industry, which allows him to repeat (in part) a development historically out of phase.

Praising the chains?

His greatest talent as a story-teller lies perhaps in the way he can give his material the shape of an apparently inescapable, fatal logic. This logic may be false somewhere: it is after all the overwhelming chain of miseries, humiliations and defeats seen from the point of view of the eternal victim, in a world where even the oppressors are shown to be victims. It almost amounts to a form of apologetics for leaving things as they are. But what his critics have been quick to spot as a mystification, the endless litany of victimisation, accompanied by a lugubrious celebration of despair ('the gesture of impotence'), is in another sense the craftsman's delight in creating ever more perfectly constructed vicious circles. In this case, the films are autobiographical in a very straightforward manner: they translate into fictional terms and formal configurations the personal experience of film-making. Having to overproduce in order to produce at all suggests the vicious circle of capitalist logic. Having to sell himself as an independent producer to those with money, the state, to the press, the public, while at the same time having to manipulate and exploit others to extract from them their loyalty and labour – may this not be another vicious circle: the victim who cannot escape being oppressive, the oppressor who is himself the victim? A capitalist entrepreneur in an age of monopolies, Fassbinder wants to articulate a message of utopian liberation while being himself in chains. The realism of such a cinema, and probably its radicalism, cannot be in its overt social criticism alone, important though this may be, but in the contradictions it sustains when expressing in formal terms the conditions of its existence. The films themselves offer no way out: the more Fassbinder courts his public by dramatising the agonies of social and emotional victims, the more his cinema is in danger of becoming formalistic, static inside his own perfected dramaturgy. So far he has treated his theme as a tragedy – which it is; to break the deadlock of too facile a pessimism and still make a cinema of enlightenment for a mass audience, he may have to see it also as a comedy. In the meantime, the fact that such a cinema continues to exist is Fassbinder's real achievement, and the implicit challenge that makes his work political.

Quotations are from the following interviews with Fassbinder:
'Interview: von Wilfried Wiegand', in *Rainer Werner Fassbinder* (Carl Hanser Verlag, Munich 1975)
'Rainer Werner Fassbinder' (interview by Corinna Brocher), in *Die Filmemacher,* edited by B. Bronnen and C. Brocher (C. Bertelsmann Verlag, Munich 1973)
'Müder Wunderknabe' by B. Henrichs, in *Zeit Magazin,* no. 24, 1973
'Interview mit R. W. Fassbinder', in *Der Tagesspiegel,* 29 September 1969
'Interview über *Liebe ist kälter als der Tod',* in *Frankfurter Allgemeine Zeitung,* 26 June 1969.

Afterword
Murder, Merger, Suicide:
The Politics of *Despair*

Thomas Elsaesser

'Why, dammit, do people always want to confuse the class-struggle with the ass-struggle?'

Ralph Ellison

Since 'A Cinema of Vicious Circles' was written, several things have happened to Fassbinder's career: from a German boy-wonder with an underground reputation abroad he has made it almost to the ranks of the bankables in the international film industry. His original mini-studio-system has become less incestuous; some who made their reputation with him have left and now work elsewhere. It was the première of *Despair* at the Cannes Festival in May 1978 that endorsed the change. From the pens of journalists flowed a roll-call of great names: equal to Bergman, Buñuel, Resnais or Visconti, Fassbinder had 'overnight' become a European art-film director. With *Despair*, the sawdust and tinsel glamour of his earlier work became the real glamour of multi-million budgets and solid production values; the script was written by Tom Stoppard, a celebrity second only to Harold Pinter in the literary script stakes; with Dirk Bogarde and Andréa Ferreol he had stars who ensured international distribution, and this in turn meant that the shooting was in English, partly on sets built for Ingmar Bergman in Munich.

All this may seem a long way from the Fassbinder known to his early followers as a director of committed or at least controversial feature films, who wanted to politicise commercial cinema by educating his audiences. It seems as if my prediction that 'as the memories and direct quotations of Hollywood fade from his cinema, the public written into his films become more German' could not have been further off the mark. Fassbinder would probably argue that the political developments in West Germany over the past years, the way that terrorism has been used as a pretext to restrict certain civil liberties and build up a 'law and order' state, with direct and indirect censorship rampant in the media, have made it difficult to work on this front. The star directors of the New German Cinema all now display an intense ambivalence about German audiences, to the point where they seem to have written off the German public even if they only blame the critics. Fassbinder is perhaps the one who is most bitter about German politics, and Syberberg has launched the most outspoken campaign against German journalists and film critics. One consequence may be that directors like Fassbinder, Wenders, Herzog have no other choice but to become 'European' or international directors.

In Fassbinder's case, the problem is compounded by his mode of production. He has never been an 'independent' film-maker; his cinema is remarkable for the way it reflects and reproduces the constraints to which it owes its existence. Over the past years these constraints have not disappeared, they have merely shifted: the need to produce fast in order to produce at all has changed into a need to produce big. In his own way, he mirrors the developments of Hollywood itself, because the very momentum of big productions involves at some stage the confrontation with another public. *Despair* is in rather obvious ways designed for a particular audience, the art house crowd and festival-watchers in Europe and the United States. The question is, does this reorientation towards a public that can be wooed with art-deco nostalgia, with stars who bring their previous roles into the film, with subjects known to be fashionable – the fascist Thirties, crises of identity, middle age, difficult sex, madness and schizophrenia – does this constitute a 'sell-out' to the international art-film market, or is Fassbinder's audience-orientation now merely based on the calculation that the only serious audience for European films is a bourgeois audience? Is *Despair* an anti-art-film art-film? Certainly, it shows Fassbinder's versatility in appropriating and rewriting the stylistic idiom of the art-film genre, but it also indicates a break, and a reflection on his previous work: the central issues of his cinema are more clearly articulated, and, paradoxically, in a more radical form than in any of his overtly militant films. What the following article is concerned with, then, is to bring out some of the implications of Fassbinder's change from melodrama to art movie, and in this way to reformulate questions about the situation of his cinema.

Fassbinder's films, as I tried to argue, are about entrapment, imprisonment, double-binds. The choice of genres – first the gangster film, then the melodrama and now the format of the art-film – seems to reflect his changing understanding of the issues involved, especially as they relate to the cinema as an institution of emotional control. During the period of the melodramas, roughly from *Merchant of Four Seasons* (1971) to *Mother Küsters* (1975) and *Fox* (1975), the central motivation of the films is how to escape from the family and its substitutes, including lesbian, homosexual and political double-binds. The films consume themselves by imagining ever new ways of breaking the hold of the power-relations and exploitative mechanism of the family under capitalism, and they find their form, their point of closure, their unified perspective by asserting pessimistically the failure and impossibility of such an escape.

The melodrama was a crucial phase in formulating this problem, mainly for two reasons: it provided a rigorous narrative closure (tragedy, the vicious circles) and it problematised identity as a process of perception, the self forming itself in a struggle between 'the way the characters perceive themselves and the way that others perceive them'. The melodrama in this sense dramatises the failure of subjectivity – any subjectivity, but quite often a specifically female subjectivity – to inscribe itself permanently into the space of the fiction (the play of seeing and being seen as a conflict of forced self-images and social roles). Emotion, desire traverses the narrative as an interruption, leaving the marks of excess, in some sense irrecuperable, but none the less finally held and articulated within the conventions of classical narrative as the pathos of waste, loss and misunderstanding. The second reason for Fassbinder's 'discovery' of the melodrama was that it seemed to posit the question of identity and subjectivity in the context of socially and ideologically explicit family or sexual relationships. From a perspective of realism, melodrama appeared progressive for bringing together and pointing out connections between three different spaces usually isolated from each other: the social space of the middle class, the physical space of the home and the small-town community, and the emotional space of the family. In other words, the melodrama implicitly challenges the split and separation between public and private, so fundamental to bourgeois ideology, and thus towards the end of an era it rejoins a problematic dating back to the eighteenth century and the rise of bourgeois tragedy.

However, radical though it may be to pinpoint the repressive effects of family, class and economic exploitation in the German context, recourse to the melodrama does not in itself amount to a political perspective, and Fassbinder made himself many enemies among the German left when he seemed to be saying in films such as *Fox* or *Mother Küsters* that left-wing politics and capitalism are not so different when it comes to emotional exploitation and identity crises. And this conclusion may have been recognised by Fassbinder himself as a false alternative, entailed by the form, and his melodramas will probably appear as transitional formulations of a position where sexual politics become the key to class or party politics. Moving on from melodrama has to be seen, therefore, also in the dialectic of a dialogue with the German student (bourgeois) left, and it constitutes a radicalisation in Fassbinder's apparent insistence that the problems of sexual identity and subjectivity have to be represented differently, that even the pessimism of the closed form, the 'vicious circle', has to be displaced, rephrased.

What Fassbinder turned to was not comedy (*Satan's Brew*, 1976, seems something of a sport, an attempt at absurdist melodrama), but a genre where the problem of identity has a long history: the European art film, at least since *Marienbad*, *8½*, *Persona*, is preoccupied with the bourgeois ego, the split personality, the divided self, the reality of the mind, etc. *Despair* aligns itself with this tradition: its setting and social context are unmistakably upper middle class, and it is even, unlike the book from which the story is taken, historically located – between 1930 and 1932. But the narrative articulation, as in Buñuel or Resnais, shifts this ideologically and historically defined material into what one might call, provisionally, a symbolic realm: the plot is hard to follow, the narrative sequence seems structured according to some 'invisible logic', the principles of intelligibility have to be constructed by the spectator. Analysing human relationships under capitalism for Fassbinder now involves a critique of realist narrative and didactic fiction. The emphasis is on the modes and dynamics of subjectivity in the filmic discourse as it involves the spectator directly, in the act of seeing and of being placed by the film. For instance, one would wish to know why the European art cinema has shown an increasing distrust of depth of field shots, and in Fassbinder in particular why this has led to extensive use of rack-focus and zoom, and those many scenes where the picture plane is flattened by shooting at right angles to a wall or arranging the figures in a frontal position. Could it be that the inscription of the subject is no longer a matter of placing a character *in* the fiction, in the space of perspectival representation? Rather than define characters by the degree to which they participate in or act upon events, what counts is their relationship to the screen, how they figure in the constantly created and rearranged field that fixes positions for characters, audience and camera.

One way to put it would be to say that *Despair*, like Nabokov's novel, reflects the general question of the status of fictional characters, the disjuncture between individuality and identity familiar from the modernist novel. Or it could be said that Fassbinder's films are changing from realistic parables into self-referential, self-reflexive films. Neither seems quite satisfactory, and especially the latter notion needs to be explained further. For one thing, the melodramas are in a sense as 'self-reflexive' or distanced as *Despair* is stylised, and for another, the closure in Fassbinder's melodramas often did not fulfil the role it plays in classical narrative: to give, in the unity and completeness of the fiction, an imaginary unity to the spectator, to allow him in the spectacle of tragedy or pathos a fixed position – that on the side of the victim – where feeling and understanding, subjectivity and consciousness would be rejoined in the knowledge that the enigma had been resolved, the loose ends tied up. In Fassbinder this unity of the spectator is achieved only at a price: it involves further distanciation, stylisation, ironies, excesses, and a *mise en scène* that underscores the 'constructed' nature of these endings, the sense that the unity of the fiction is the result of artifice.

In the symbolic relations created by the narrative of *Despair*, the hero embodies well enough a central preoccupation of the European art cinema, namely under what conditions can the bourgeois subject, the individual, be unified, contained, reinserted into the discourse of his or her society, a discourse which allows for few positions outside: only that of madness or total solipsism. But *Despair* also embodies the Fassbinder themes of imprisonment and escape. Based on Nabokov's émigré novel, first published in 1936, which is treated both faithfully and very liberally, the story concerns Hermann Hermann, a chocolate manufacturer of Russian origin, living in Berlin with his empty-headed, flirtatious wife and her cousin, a pseudo-bohemian painter who is having an affair with Hermann's wife and is scrounging off an income that is rapidly depleted as Hermann's family business slides into bankruptcy. After an unsuccessful attempt at negotiating a business merger, Hermann happens to meet at a fairground mirror-maze a vagrant in whom he detects a perfect resemblance to himself. Over the subsequent weeks or months he hatches a plan, whereby he bribes Felix, the vagrant, into putting on his clothes and acting as his double. Felix finally accepts, is then shot by Hermann, who had instructed his wife, after telling her about a mysterious, criminal brother, to collect Hermann's life insurance premium and join him in Switzerland. The scheme fails, mainly because the police have no reason to believe the dead man to be Hermann, since there is in actual fact little resemblance between the two. A clue left at the scene of the crime gives away the identity of the victim, and it is merely a matter of time until Hermann, now living under Felix's name, is tracked down by the police in his Alpine retreat. The film ends with him making a speech on his arrest, in which he claims to be an actor playing a criminal.

Such are the bare bones of the plot. The manner in which Fassbinder presents the action, however, makes it at first sight near incomprehensible to anyone who has not read the book. Fantasy scenes and 'reality' are mixed indiscriminately, without any difference in the manner of representation. Also, the fact that the narrative progression, as involuted as in the original, though in a different way, is not governed by action time or any other kind of psychological time makes the film appear slow-moving, static, and to many viewers exasperatingly boring. But if a first viewing gives the sense of a lavish but somewhat erratic adaptation, from which no clear narrative voice or voices emerge, a second viewing suggests that the logic of the narrative is dephased or disjointed in order to bring out a structure which, though present in Nabokov's novel, is considerably tightened and organised with a different problem in mind.

Hermann's predicament in the film, in one word, is impotence: primarily sexual, but also economic and political. The film recounts his struggle to cope with this feeling, in confrontations taking place at his office, with his wife, talking to the painter cousin, at a business meeting with his rival, in an outdoor café. But to call 'impotence' what unites these obliquely presented episodes is to state much too boldly the dilemma that the narrative is designed to explore, namely what exactly it is that makes the discovery of his double and the plan to switch identities an alternative and a way out for Hermann. In an obvious sense, he is another Fassbinder hero who feels trapped and who plots escape: the escape traps him further and more decisively. As in Sophocles' *Oedipus*, destiny manifests itself in the movement to evade it. But what singles Hermann out is his reluctance to be drawn into the game that assigns to him the role of jealous husband, or to act out the triangle made up of himself, Lydia his wife, and Ardalion, her lover. So reluctant is he in fact that he represses all knowledge of her incestuous adultery, and instead imagines himself a masterful and irresistible mate. In one of the scenes where he surprises the two together in Ardalion's studio loft, he is frantically searching for nothing more appropriately inappropriate than one of Ardalion's 'excruciatingly bad' paintings, representing a briar pipe and two apples, but which turns out to be an ashtray and two roses.

The repression is not without consequences: Hermann experiences a split, a 'dissociation', and at night is given to watching himself make love to his wife, as he sits or sees himself sitting at the other end of the hallway. This phenomenon of seeing himself double is the initial form that his dilemma takes. But it follows what is essentially the first scene in the film, where his wife, naked, moves towards him, her left arm raised, provocatively spraying her shaven armpit with perfume. The scene can be seen as a metonymic representation of the threat that runs throughout the film: the display of 'nothing there' in the context of sexual desire. Lydia's gaze invites his, but he responds by stepping protectively behind a voluminous armchair. To put it like this, however, is to make a correlation between shot and countershot which the film actually interrupts with a marked spatial dislocation. There is no eye-contact, not even negative, between the two characters: both glance directly into the camera, but each shot is held too long to produce a closure of the visual field, nor is there a cutback to Lydia. It is the spectator who has to make a choice of either bridging the gap that the *mise en scène* opens up, or – and this is of some importance – of constructing the spatial coherence in a different sense, for instance by treating the camera as another character.

Elsewhere, Lydia's appetite recalls to Hermann that of his mother 'stuffing chocolates into her silly face'. Members of the 'Viennese delegation' (Nabokov's phrase) will have no trouble in diagnosing a pathological inability to master the incestuous feelings towards his mother, transferred to Lydia via the incestuous Ardalion: feelings so strongly disavowed as to make him impotent. Shaven armpit or briar pipe, Fassbinder (aided by Nabokov) gives generous indications towards the underlying structure of this disavowal: to search for the briar pipe is to negate the threat represented by the armpit, in order to substitute for the lack a fetish object that can represent it symbolically.

This is the structure in which Felix figures as the double: in one sense a substitute for the briar pipe picture never found, and in another sense the narcissistic alternative to the paranoid double vision of watching himself watching. Felix is what Hermann is not: young, strong, free of family or social obligations, and he voices what Hermann cannot admit: that women are fickle, deceitful, adulterous. By changing places with Felix, Hermann can put himself in the position of a successful husband without having to fulfil the role. By negating, liquidating his social persona, by slipping out from under all the impossible demands, he can exchange a faltering identity for a fixed one, controlled and circumscribed by the negation of his former self from which it springs. The murder of Felix is a suicide, of the kind known from Kafka's story *The Judgment*. Hermann can punish himself in the act of shooting Felix, assuming the role of dominance and submission simultaneously. By shooting a substitute, he eliminates his own inadequate self, to be reborn, on the other side of the border, in 'neutral' Switzerland, and live the life of (virile?) independence rather than castrated misogyny. The kind of revenge Hermann fantasises is illustrated by the story he tells his wife about the allegedly criminal brother: he poisoned his mistress. (It makes her the symmetrical equivalent to the chocolate-eating mother.) For obvious reasons, the shooting of Felix is a crucial scene. It is shown twice, to bring out the simultaneity and the contradiction of the two positions, in a *mise en scène* that illustrates Fassbinder's approach to filmic space. It is crucial also in that the homosexual component of the narrative is used as a kind of intermediary structure between two impossibilities. The process of transforming Felix into Hermann is shown as a progress of love, expressed in gesture, physicality, exchange: close-ups of hands, feet, ears, neck, scalp, toes, as Hermann trims, shaves, pedicures and washes Felix before dressing him in his clothes, underscore a heavily eroticised ritual, a love-making which the fatal shot in the back consummates. The murder comes as a point of relief, and Hermann's divided self fuses momentarily in the image of love and death mutually experienced.

As Hermann fires the shot, Fassbinder frames Felix in medium close-up looking into the camera, and almost inaudibly he whispers 'Thank you' as he sinks down. The ringing of the shot is overlaid with the ringing of the doorbell in Lydia's apartment; in rapid succession we see the police investigation, the funeral, Lydia being paid the insurance premium. Finally Lydia, dressed in white, is seen coming towards the camera with open arms, calling Hermann's name, as he stands, also in white, with his back to her on a bridge by Lake Geneva. When he turns round it is Felix, not Hermann, but Lydia seems not to mind and the two embrace passionately. We realise that the scene has been a flash-forward, a wish-fulfilling fantasy scenario, in which the plot is doubly successful: the police fall for it, and Lydia has accepted the substitution. Felix does indeed replace Hermann at her side, and she authenticates the switch by taking him as her lover: female desire has been focused again, and thereby contained. The duplicity of the scene lies not only in the fact that it is 'imagined'; it is a subjective, point of view scene, but one in which the marks of this subjectivity are like Jakobson's grammatical shifters running through and across the characters. Beginning with Hermann's point of view (split between visual image in background and Felix's 'Thank you' in the aural foreground), the scene changes to Lydia's point of view via a complex field, made up by a series of glances exchanged between the detective, Ardalion's portrait of Hermann, and the insurance broker, a series of male glances in which Lydia figures as the product, the result, the mediator that brings the spectator to Felix's face looking at the camera and signifying the erasure of Hermann. Thematically, we are given Hermann's vision of his after-life, except that in terms of narrative expectations Felix appears where Hermann should be. The scene is thus a series of transfers and substitutions, in which Hermann's subjectivity is cut completely loose from any notion of coherent character, investing the whole of the fictional space and assuming an exalted omnipresence. That it is an impossible escape from his predicament is confirmed by cutting back to the scene of the shooting in the woods. The camera set-up is now different, we no longer have a close-up of Felix's face, there is no beatific expression or any whispered words. The sequence of events stops with the detective glancing at the portrait and disclosing that the man found dead is merely wearing Hermann's clothes and holding his passport: no further resemblance.

Does this mean that to break out of the bind Hermann would have to be Felix and Hermann, interchangeably and simultaneously? Bourgeois individuality, represented by Hermann, emerges as an irresolvable contradiction, and the double is merely the figure whereby this contradictory inscription of subjectivity is realised in the fiction. In one sense, Felix *is* the 'solution' to the dual constraint of public and private self (unsuccessful businessman and impotent husband, what more appealing subject to identify with for a middle-class, middle-aged audience?). But in contrast to the melodramas that precede *Despair*, where a line of direct identification is built up for spectators unlikely ever to see the films (e.g., the Emmis and Alis of West Germany), Fassbinder forgoes direct identification and does not attempt to unite the twofold inscription in a single character or a single, closed, narrative space (hence, on the most basic level, the coexistence of fantasy and 'real' scenes). The contradiction involved in the attempted fusion of Hermann and Felix is resolved on a different level altogether, and in such a way that the very form of the unified narrative space appears as an aberration, an impossible and repressive unification of the subject.

The radicalism of *Despair* in respect to other Fassbinder films is thus that it undercuts the opposition between actual families and surrogate families, so typical of the melodramas, by a different kind of literalism. This takes primarily the form of 'acting out' the scenario which represents Hermann's dilemma: he creates a double, a stand-in and scapegoat, another self that both compensates and expiates for the 'real' self. But such literalism makes Hermann a criminal and an outcast. To act on one's desires, especially if they are the negative pressures of social and sexual demands, is to put oneself outside the law: this, in a sense, is the most immediately accessible, banal message of the film, a re-working of the central contradiction in all Fassbinder's films about sexuality and politics. This is why the film reinserts Hermann's dilemma into another context, which makes his strategy seem both a critique and an extension of that context. Hermann's retreat from the 'family romance' into alternately paranoid and narcissistic symptomatology, with its implied consequence of madness, is construed on another level as a political act whose ultimate term is exile.

Fassbinder's allusions to Nazism have been criticised, mainly by those who know Nabokov, as a gratuitous vulgarisation and travesty of the original's restraint, given that all these scenes had to be added to the script. But this is to overlook the political implications of Nabokov's novel, and more directly to ignore how deeply politics are embedded in the film. Nazism appears as both the reverse side and the complementary aspect of Hermann's private hell: to contract out of the sexual and social demands and to split into a paranoid/narcissistic self is in the film symmetrically related to contracting into monopoly capitalism, fascism and Hitler. The narrative pointedly aligns a sexual crisis (Hermann's marriage), an economic crisis (the 'family firm' that Hermann has inherited can only be salvaged by a merger) and a political crisis (the floundering of the Weimar Republic and the emergence of the National Socialists).

Two figures in whom Hermann mirrors his own options are Müller, his production manager, and the director of the rival chocolate firm. In both cases, the conversation revolves round the politics of the day, to which Hermann can only reply with private confessions, in one case about his mother, and to the chocolate manufacturer about living with forged papers. An SA sympathiser, Müller is clearly paranoid about foreigners, Jews, the Versailles Treaty, and to allay his fears he involves himself in the Nazi party. Müller, in other words, chooses Hitler as his double, and when he appears at the office dressed in an SA uniform, the analogy with Hermann (exchanging clothes, switching roles and identities) is made evident. However, the connection works more subtly when Müller is first introduced. The morning after Hermann has been watching himself making love to his wife, she drives him to work in their limousine. Hermann, in the car, plays seductively with the hem of her skirt to expose some thigh, and busies himself on her gloved fingers: in the context of the previous night's debacle, the scene functions as a fetishisation and substitution for the potency he failed to muster (the close-ups are inversely matched by the subsequent close-ups of Hermann manicuring Felix). They kiss, and Hermann goes up the steps to his office, not without casting a miserable glance back at Lydia, who immediately checks her face and mouth in the rear view mirror of the car in a gesture which recalls (as does the armpit) Buñuel's heroine in *Un Chien Andalou*. We cut to a shot inside the office where Müller, looking out, is actually looking at his own reflection and straightening his tie as he sees his boss arrive. This gesture is symmetrically related to Lydia checking her mouth – both assure themselves of their sexuality in a specifically narcissistic and fetishising manner – and Hermann, who is outside the system of their mirror-glances, acts as the deferment that brings the gestures in relation. He is the mirror in whose reflection they compensate for the lack they perceive in him. The subsequent scenes, where Hermann and Müller talk politics, end with Hermann's face reflected in the glass partition of the inner office, with Müller's face in profile superimposing itself across the glass pane from inside.

The discussion with the rival chocolate manufacturer, after establishing verbally an analogy between chocolates and German politics (!), is primarily developed on a visual plane in which background and foreground, inside and outside are systematically juxtaposed. The scene shows the manufacturer directly challenging Hermann's identity ('Is Hermann your first name or your surname?'), and it ends with Hermann caught (and breaking down) in an elaborate play on political colours ('a Blackshirt fighting the Reds in the White Army, then I fought the Brownshirts in the Red Army, and all I am now is a yellowbelly in a brown trade [or: tide?]'): brown is the emblematic colour of a false identity (politics, repressed homosexuality, business) from which the only escape is exile. On the visual plane, the conversation is doubled by the factory assembly line, which turns out little brown men in chocolate, all replicas, veritable choc-troops of political doubles, ending like piled-up corpses in a box marked rejects. Fassbinder's image of the fascist state as exploiting the double-bind of narcissism and paranoia considerably deepens a passage in the book where Nabokov's Hermann explains the political significance of the double in terms that recall, more than anything else, a scene from Lang's *Metropolis*:

> It even seems to me that my basic theme, the resemblance between two persons, has a profound allegorical meaning. [. . .] In fancy, I visualize a new world, where all men will resemble one another as Hermann and Felix did; a world of Helixes and Fermanns; a world where the worker fallen dead at the

feet of his machine will be at once replaced by his perfect double smiling the serene smile of perfect socialism. (V. Nabokov, *Despair*, Weidenfeld & Nicholson, 1965)

Nabokov, in this passage, seems to distance himself derisively from his narrator. Fassbinder, who takes his hero more seriously, uses the assembly line as a metaphor for the imbrication of capitalism, paranoia and the fascist state. This connection between private and public is reiterated in the scene where Hermann, about to seal the letter which will bribe Felix into donning Hermann's clothes, hesitates as he watches just such a line of brownshirts hurling bricks at the window of a Jewish butcher's shop. Their frustration at not being able to smash the window (rhyming as it does with an earlier scene where Müller beats his fists against the wall in the office) acts as a relay in Hermann's mind for the decision he is about to take, Felix now figuring explicitly to fill the space left by a political impasse as well as the personal one; or, to put it differently, Hermann's presence at the scene, his gaze, inscribes his dilemma into the specifically historical space of nascent Nazism.

The economic dimension, in so far as it revolves round an analysis of fascism as the extreme political form of monopoly capitalism, an analysis actualised by the decline of Hermann's family firm, enters the narrative in a peculiarly compressed and condensed play on words: a pun on merger/murder, twice repeated. Fusion and aggressivity, the merging of identities and of businesses, which involves a murder that is suicide, a police state that will eventually destroy a nation. The extreme condensation which Fassbinder here employs to make the private intersect with the economic and political does not altogether redeem what to the casual viewer will merely seem a bad and laboured pun (of the kind well-known to readers of Stoppard), but it does allow for a reformulation of the paradigm that seems to generate the narrative and determines the elliptical and fragmented segmentation of the story-line. Hermann's dilemma is founded on a double negation, structured symmetrically: to the disavowal of his wife's adultery corresponds the disavowal of any difference between himself and Felix. The two acts of repression (murder and merger, 'threat of castration' and 'denial of difference') confront each other as mirrors, and the paranoia associated with the former is countered with a continually renewed temptation, at once consummated and forever barred with the murder of Felix, to 'regress' to total narcissism. Hermann resorts to this solution after realising that the world around him is caught in the same trap of the paranoiac/narcissistic double bind.

It is this position, so common in Fassbinder's melodramas, that the 'self-reflexivity' of the art-film attempts to clarify and overcome. Thus far, the narrative has been analysed in terms of an explicitly Oedipal logic, centred on 'castration-anxiety' as the term that focuses the contradictory paradigm of overvaluing and undervaluing difference. More concretely, the narrative's oscillation between paranoia and narcissism could be construed as the consequence of repressed homosexuality, although such a formulation would again suggest that the film is primarily concerned with the pathology of the main protagonist.

However, *Despair* actually structures disavowal in terms of a defective or partial vision. One might say that the logic of the film implies that *because* Hermann doesn't recognise what is going on between Lydia and Ardalion, he is over-anxious to discover similarity between Felix and himself. But if this is so, then another structure, more basic, about recognition and miscognition, about vision and point of view in general, underpins and determines the narrative as analysed above, and which also turns on paranoia and narcissism, castration and difference. In other words, the logic that articulates the plot, and might account for the deviations and dislocations of *Despair* when compared to the 'realist' film, is itself dictated by the nature of cinematic representation and identification, which it investigates and problematises.

I have talked about *Despair* as if the film ended soon after Hermann shoots Felix in the woods. It doesn't. Whereas it is true that Lydia disappears virtually with the flash-forward that shows her accept Felix as Hermann, the latter's flight to Switzerland is a process first of physical deterioration and decay, but also almost literally a 'falling to pieces'. Most striking are the scenes at the Swiss hotel where his false position and false identity, his silence, make him an object in other people's speculations, a fragment in their discourse. The process culminates in a shot that shows a shattered mirror, shards of a broken washbowl, and Hermann's hand holding into the frame a passport with Felix's photo. This résumé of the plot, a visual reminder to the artifice that makes up his identity, is juxtaposed with a particularly graphic 'return of the repressed': the clue left at the scene of the crime, and which points to Felix's identity (and thereby Hermann's), is a solid, carved walking stick; and Hermann's manic laughter when he discovers how the police are being led to his hideout is that of a man who has also read his Freud. The Oedipal trap seems to open only on to a series of interminable and potentially endless substitutions for the initial configuration: briar-pipes, lipsticks, walking-sticks – so many fetish objects circulating within the narrative. The film has no closure in terms of the dilemma it poses, and while on the surface it moves towards the false ending of the police thriller (detection and capture), psychologically Hermann is condemned to endless repetition, and narrative space becomes the mirror-maze.

What happens is that Fassbinder shifts the problem to another level. The limited form of self-reference embodied in the non-realist discourse is deconstructed in the final scene, when Hermann steps out of his room to make his speech of surrender and abdication. The fragmented composition gives way to a frontal shot, a direct stare. But the speech itself and the stare have to be read, within the fictional framework, as the sign that Hermann is now insane, believing in earnest the story he had been telling Felix about needing him as an understudy. However, Hermann's terminal madness, the violent unification outside society, outside the law, takes the shape of thinking of himself as an actor in a film: which is exactly what Bogarde/Hermann is.

This tilt of the fiction, whereby madness in the story proper turns out to be the truth of the cinema when considered literally, cheats the spectator of a resolution, disorients or disappoints, not least because his presence is demanded by the film in a much more abrupt way. The new form of address entails a particular position, a stance, a perspective, but it is not the one that one expects from a fiction film, where narrative closure reconciles the spectator to his own split self by giving him the experience of unity, of understanding. In *Despair*, however, the rupture is not as sudden as all that. Throughout, the kind of alternation involved in the various processes of identifying with the main character, for instance, is systematically blocked and disrupted. In particular, the narrativisation of the split between identifying with the look *of* the character and the look *at* the character, typical of classical narrative, is forestalled for a number of precise reasons. Most fundamentally, as spectators we instantly notice that Felix is no physical double of Hermann, which eliminates one kind of suspense and puts us at an advantage over the hero. The audience's position of knowledge in this instance is exaggerated, overplayed to the point where one is likely to be exasperated or puzzled by his 'mistake'. One either loses interest or has to look elsewhere to explain Hermann's *idée fixe*. Secondly, Hermann's gaze does not act as a focus for our attention. His motivation remains obscure, his desire is not evident from the movement of the plot itself: both the sexual and the economic motive are indirectly presented, and the lure we are given in their place, financial gain from an insurance swindle, hardly satisfies. This lack of apparent motivation affects the audience's response to Lydia, whose occasional nudity is offered to the spectator's gaze, but at no point valorised by male desire. Nor does she exist 'in her own right' as a centre of motivation. Her presence is negated by making her silly, a walking parody of the alluring female. What intervenes between the look and its object, as in the opening scene, is the camera as an unlocalised immaterial character, a substitute, but covering neither the spectator's point of view nor that of the protagonist. Lastly, the few times we see events from Hermann's perspective, this vantage point is undermined by the fact that his vision is shown to be defective regarding crucial elements of the narrative: he sees too little and too much.

In this respect, *Despair* reformulates quite radically what has perhaps been the most significant and original feature of Fassbinder's style from *Katzelmacher* onwards. The split of the spectator's point of view mentioned above, on the basis of which films construct the congruence between subjectivity and knowledge, has always been dephased or disjointed in Fassbinder. Instead of adopting the narrative system of delegating, circulating and exchanging the look of the camera across the visual field of the characters, the spectator and the absent observer (thus creating a homogeneous narrative space), Fassbinder has tended to privilege or exaggerate one axis over the others, mainly by three types of shots and the figurations they produce. Frontal shots of characters looking (glance-object shots) but without shots of what the character looks at; tableau-like static compositions which by their very symmetry 'cite' an invisible observer (which has to be the 'real' audience, because the shots are never claimed by any of the characters within the film, and because they are organised around what one might call an internal frame, accentuating the spectator perspective; finally, inversely related to the previous type, shots where another spectator perspective is constructed within the action, through a character or characters whose main function it is to observe and who, as it were, 'anchor' the scene by their presence and gaze, most notably perhaps, the figure of Marlene in *The Bitter Tears of Petra von Kant*.

The point of this defective *suture* in Fassbinder has always been twofold: to make his characters' dilemma a function of their roles and self-images, as if to say, these people only behave like this because they are being looked at, but if they weren't looked at they would not exist. And secondly, to implicate the spectator in this as a third term whose presence can be inscribed and activated, instead of being merely given.

The paradox of Emmi and Ali, for instance, in *Fear Eats the Soul*, could be described as grounded in the fact that they cannot be 'seen together', because there is no social space (work, leisure, family) in which their liaison is tolerated: they are the objects of extremely aggressive and hostile voyeurism. But conversely, they cannot exist without being seen *by others*, for when they are alone they fail to find fixed positions; the mutually sustaining gaze is no substitute for wanting to be confirmed in the gaze of others, a gaze they seek eventually, and thus compromise themselves. The final shot resolves the paradox by showing the doctor in the hospital fixing benevolent eyes on them, but it is a look which we, the spectators, see in a mirror that is placed parallel to the plane of the camera. In other words, the need/impossibility of being perceived by others and still remaining a subject produces both the sickness and the cure (the wish-fulfilling regression to a pure mother/son, nurse/invalid relationship under the eyes of an institutionally benevolent, sanitised father); but it is a relation that only the spectator can read, because he alone perceives the configuration of this tableau, thanks to the placing of the mirror, through which he is inscribed in the scene as another benevolent but also 'knowing' gaze.

Likewise, in *Petra von Kant*, it is the silent observer Marlene who anchors in the place of the mirror the space of which the spectator is the other mooring point. Her presence in the background doubles the spectator's shadowy existence in the implied foreground, a position accentuated by the theatrical 'proscenium' space created by filming at right angles to the picture plane. The section where Marlene is absent throws into relief her function: this occurs on Petra's *birth*day when she has a nervous breakdown, and it represents the absence of control, the moment of excess, of totally fragmented and dispersed subjectivity which produces (and is produced by) the visit from her mother and daughter, the visible return of repressed and displaced conflicts. However, this section, it has been remarked, follows most closely the compositional rules of the point-of-view shot, of eye-contact and of psychological space as known from classical narrative. Fassbinder seems to be identifying 'cinematic realism' with the presence of actual families, as in the melodramas. *Petra von Kant* ends when Marlene, asked to give up her role of the silent gaze and enter into the sphere of words, walks out rather than speak.

What is characteristic of these two films, and others, is that the treatment of space, the *mise en scène*, is directly determined by the problems raised in the narrative; in particular, the possibility or impossibility of breaking out of the charmed family circle. In the absence of a stable identity within the family (and all Fassbinder films show why such a stability is impossible), the need to be perceived, to be confirmed, becomes paramount as the structure that regulates and at the same time disturbs the articulations of subjectivity. This means that the cinema itself, as a place where the look is traded, becomes the agency that can confirm a structure of identity outside the family, that can and does in fact act as a substitute family, an alternative (to) Oedipus. The question is, for whom?

It is this implicit question that *Despair* formulates explicitly. Fassbinder has, it seems, adopted the fashionable techniques of the art-movie to restructure and rearticulate the thematic-formal core of his own cinema. What in the previous films was largely a matter of presenting the spectator with mirrors of himself as a voyeuristic presence, now is a matter of analysing more fundamental relations. The breakdown of identification described above leads to a form of dissociation that is not merely another 'distancing device'. An example from the film might clarify the point. At one stage Hermann and Ardalion are engaged in a discussion of Lydia at a restaurant. The scene is initially framed as an over-the-shoulder two-shot with Hermann facing in the general direction of Ardalion and the camera. Ardalion's back fills the left-hand side of the frame. The camera then starts a slow travelling shot to the right, which we have to read as a subjective shot from Ardalion's point of view. As Hermann continues to talk, the camera has become stationary and suddenly Ardalion re-enters the frame, but not, as expected, from the left where we last saw him, to 'claim' the point-of-view shot; instead he enters from behind Hermann, on the right, and Fassbinder cuts at just the moment when Ardalion completely obliterates Hermann in the frame. The point here is not that Hermann has been talking to himself, but that Ardalion has, as it were, delegated his look to the spectator via the camera and thereby marked as a conspicuous absence the point of view of the spectator. Hermann's predicament is that Ardalion has 'set him up' just as Fassbinder has set us up.

In the same scene Hermann is talking about his dissociations to a man he believes to be a psychoanalyst whom Ardalion has introduced to him, against the background of one of Ardalion's paintings depicting a village in the Alps. It turns out that the stranger is an insurance broker, and Hermann has once again been duped into living in a world set up and controlled by Ardalion. In just this way the shots where the camera forces the spectator to claim a point of view not motivated internally by a character are moments of dissociation where the imaginary identity of the spectator as invisible observer is called into question. They challenge us with an absence that cannot be repressed. Hermann, on the other hand, is in a similar position. A symbolic absence is being disavowed, filled with mirrors and substitutions: he, too, comes to face that absence head-on in the final address to the spectator, which is the point at which the spectator is forced to realise that the film as fiction only exists by virtue of fundamental repression — that of the awareness of the camera as camera, of audience as audience, of actor as actor. Fassbinder thus operates another reduction, a literalisation of the film itself into the terms of the viewing situation.

On the face of it, Hermann's speech is taken almost directly from Nabokov's novel:

> Hold the policemen, knock them down, sit on them. A famous film actor will come running out of this house. He is an arch criminal but he must escape. I want you to make a free passage for him. I want a clean getaway. That's all. I'm coming out. (cf. *Despair*, Weidenfeld & Nicholson, 1965, p. 222)

Fassbinder must have been pleased to find this passage. History has added a meaning to the final sentence that even Nabokov might not have anticipated: Hermann doesn't just come out of the house, he also comes out of the narrative into another space, and out of the Oedipal configuration coded as repressed homosexuality. And so Fassbinder added a line to Nabokov's text. Before the frame freezes on the words 'I'm coming out', Hermann says: 'Don't look at the camera', and with this act of naming, Hermann comes out of being a character in a self-contained fiction. The shot frames Hermann/Bogarde's face looking into the camera, and at its edges the barrels of guns are visible, though not those who hold them, since we as audience are placed in this position.

With Hermann's speech, the film attains its closure by substituting one frame of reference for another. The triangular relationships of Lydia/Ardalion/Hermann-Felix are replaced by another triangle made up of actor/camera/spectator-identity, explicitly named and thereby terminating the fiction. If Hermann (whom the murder of Felix and exile have reduced to silence, denial of identity and the role of being a figure in the hotel guests' conversation) attains an identity on the side of madness, this madness also allows him to reappropriate the word as the final gesture of a successful substitution. For the shifting subject positions which I analysed in the fantasy scene do not stop with the transformation of Hermann into Felix; they continue until they 'literalise' the actor. Whether the process stops here or whether it implicates, as it must, the director himself, is a further problem. The point to repeat, perhaps, is that *Despair* involves two kinds of literalisation: it deconstructs the melodrama in so far as it represents the process of doubling and splitting directly, and it deconstructs cinematic representation by naming the camera as the term which is in play between actor and spectator.

What does this indicate? Hermann's madness, which, to quote the German title, is a 'journey into light', unifies him outside the law (the 'arch criminal') in a position which equates the enigma *in* the narrative — who is Hermann, what is his problem? — with the enigma *of* the narrative — what is the function of a fiction film? Lifting the fundamental repression at the end means abandoning the space of the cinema as a psychological or ideological institution, for it cancels the system of fetishisations and substitutions that generate the narrative in the first place. The fiction itself is the lack which the cinema both covers up and fetishises for the benefit of the spectator (but also for Hermann: the film opens with the words '... all these things we have lost forever'). Yet, as it turns out, the structure which is named as underpinning the Oedipal motivation of the narrative, the triangle of actor, camera, spectator, is – from the spectator's point of view – subject to the same instability of paranoia and narcissism as the story of Hermann which it concludes: the narcissism and paranoia of the plot find their congruence in the voyeurism and identification mechanisms whereby the fiction film constitutes itself as coherent, as a unity, as an object. This is what is put in crisis in *Despair*: the fictional character, at the point at which he avows himself to be an actor, turns out to be the 'paranoid' construction of the spectator, because Fassbinder's peculiar *mise en scène*, his use of the false point-of-view shot and of spatial dislocation, in effect bars the narcissistic compensation of paranoia that seals identification in the classical narrative.

We can paraphrase the process by allegorising *Despair* as a discourse about identification in the classical text: it represents the spectator, who 'murders' the fictional character by taking him over, dressing him up in the feelings of his idealised self-image. On the other hand, the spectator commits 'suicide' in order to live (temporarily) in the actor and through him. What Hermann acts out in the murder/merger paradigm are less 'his' fantasies, but the spectator's, and Fassbinder has literalised the ontological position of the spectator *vis à vis* the screen by indicating its pathological side. Or to phrase it the other way round: the pathology of the bourgeois subject today mirrors the ontology of the institution cinema and the construction of the classical narrative text. The two interlock and mutually predicate each other. To simplify the equation: Felix is to Hermann what Hermann is to the spectator – the Other that is made into the Same, at a cost of considerable violence and repression. Felix functions as the Fetish, the substitute for the ultimate signifier in this system, the condition for the unification of the subject, and the guarantee for the kind of pleasure that *Despair* seems to frustrate. This is why Felix, not Lydia, is the object of desire, but why at the same time this desire has to be repressed. The logic seems to be that cinematic pleasure is fundamentally narcissistic, and where narrative codifies male desire, it is bound to articulate a covertly homosexual text.

Hermann's escape from the confines of the family triangle is thus paradigmatically related to the function of the cinema as escapism, the fiction filling an absence with the sign that connotes this absence. To say that the cinema is escapist entertainment and functions socially as a means of containing the 'threat of castration' is to say that characters, stars, actors, but also narrative itself, exist in order to disavow incompleteness or the anxiety of incompleteness experienced by the spectator; an incompleteness that the camera and editing transform into the repetition of absence and presence, which is the rhythm of narrative. The defectiveness of *Despair* as a classical text is precisely what allows it to deconstruct that text, in the guise of a plea for sexual liberation against the background of heterosexual misery and fascism.

The final image, on one level, brings together representation and that which is represented: nothing is there except what you see. Dedicated to Artaud, the film has come full circle at the point where the distance between actor and part has become nil, where the notion of fiction and spectacle is replaced by that of 'performance' in the minimalist-theatrical sense, as the zero degree of representation. Yet the very logic of the literalisation I have been describing implies that the author is *in* the text, but not 'behind' the characters. In a sense, the account of the ending is incomplete. The Alpine scene in which it takes place can be recognised, not without a certain shocked surprise, as the landscape prefigured in the painting of Ardalion that we see, half-finished, on the wall of the restaurant. And as the police surround Hermann's hideout one sees briefly, almost at the edge of the frame, Ardalion, with an easel, 'finishing' *his* picture. So that while in one respect Hermann is the first Fassbinder character fully to 'return the look', to address the camera head-on after having sought to appropriate it as a mirror, in another respect *Despair*, too, is a film in which the closure is achieved by leaving a substitute gaze in the frame. Fassbinder's cinema, so totally defined by the relation between image, camera and spectator, has as its 'structuring absence' also the problem of the self-representation of the author, but in the sense that his mode of presence-representation is a pure structure of perception.

If this can be localised at all, apart from the analysis I have attempted of the film, it must be formulated in terms of the split which makes both Hermann and Ardalion delegates of the author's look (as well as the spectator), while at the same time it sets them up as adversaries. Hence a certain ambiguity after all. Is Hermann's speech as he 'becomes' the actor a call to arms, an endorsement of some kind of struggle, in which the weapons that are visible at the edge of the frame are 'handed over' to the spectator? Are arms the lack which the fiction tries to compensate? Or is the actor-artist, under cover of such a suggestion, trying to 'get away'? The realisation that Hermann is coming out of the space of the narrative cinema is undercut by the knowledge that he is still in the world of Ardalion, in the space of art.

Despair is an art film, in so far as its self-reflexivity, its use of Ardalion's art as a frame-within-a-frame-within-a-frame, represents an implicit commitment to the fiction film; yet it is an anti-art art-film in so far as the impasse of Hermann's 'sexual politics' implies no great faith in the survival of this cinema outside the pathology of the bourgeois psyche and its modes of self-representation. If the cinema is a mirror, only the bourgeoisie can be reflected in it. Fassbinder is still busy showing us how much that leaves out.

Reading Fassbinder's Sexual Politics

Richard Dyer

Fassbinder's films[1] tend to provoke political debate. In *Gay Left* no. 2 there was a review by Bob Cant of *Fox and his Friends*.[2] Cant admired the film for its anatomy of 'the corruptive nature of capitalism' (not only at the general level of the film's showing that 'in a bourgeois society all relationships have economic overtones', but also in the way that, through the references to Hollywood and the scene with the GIs, the film brings out 'that West Germany – like most of Western Europe – is a neo-colony of American imperialism') and for its unflinching depiction of 'the jungle-like atmosphere' of 'the gay ghetto'. In the third issue of the journal, Andrew Britton wrote a reply to Cant's review, seeing the film as one whose 'version of homosexuality degrades us all, and should be roundly denounced'. Britton argued that the film does not deal with the impact of capitalist economic structures on human relationships but merely with a moralising view of '"filthy lucre"' and that '"people with money tend to be unpleasant"'. Moreover, the film fails, in his view, to deal with the specificities of homosexuality – both as this sexual orientation articulates with class (i.e. the different experience of middle-class and working-class gays; 'why and how the bourgeois gays depicted have come to acquiesce in the institutions of the society which oppresses them') and in the particular oppression that gay people suffer in society ('There is nothing in *Fox* to show that gayness is subject to ideological, social or legal constraints').

An echo of this exchange over *Fox*, though less focused since the writers were not specifically addressing each other, can be found in Elizabeth Wilson's account of *The Bitter Tears of Petra von Kant* in *Red Rag* no. 10 and in Caroline Sheldon's remarks on the same film in her article in *Gays and Film*. Wilson sees *Petra von Kant* as 'less about lesbianism than about women's place in society' and argues that 'throughout the film Fassbinder relates the psychological constructs of relationships to the economic realities on which they are based'. Sheldon, on the other hand, places *Petra von Kant* in the 'freak show genre' of 'men's films about lesbians', alongside *Les Biches* and *The Fox*. She sees it stressing the (implicitly inherent) 'unwholesomeness' of the women, and compares it unfavourably with *Fox and his Friends*, concluding that 'From this comparison it appears that male gay film-makers are no more sympathetic to lesbians than straight ones'.

These two pairs of exchanges crystallise the kind of debate that surrounds Fassbinder's films, especially in relation to sexual politics. Two themes in particular emerge – the relationship between class and sex politics in Fassbinder's films, and the 'unpleasantness' of the worlds the films depict. The divergence of views on these themes – which run through so much of the critical literature I shall refer to in this article – seems to me to be related to the ambiguity of the films themselves. This ambiguity can be located in the films' political perspective, which I want to designate as 'left-wing melancholy'. In the next section of this article I want to try to delineate this perspective as it informs Fassbinder's films, stressing its reactionary implications. In the final section, however, I want to move back from this analysis in a series of qualifications. In particular, I want to argue that the kind of debate exemplified by Bob Cant and Andrew Britton, Elizabeth Wilson and Caroline Sheldon, indicates the real effectivity* of Fassbinder's films, an effectivity that cannot be automatically read off from the films themselves, an effectivity moreover that the films do not, as it were, deserve.

The divergences of views outlined above are partly explicable by the ambiguity of the films at the level of dialogue and narrative. It would be very hard to determine what sense one is supposed to make of many of the films' endings, for instance. Why does Marlene leave Petra? Petra apologises to her for her habitual treatment of her; Marlene kisses Petra's hand, and the latter snaps, 'Not like that!', and it is at this point that Marlene starts to pack her bag. Petra's response to Marlene's gesture is the kind of opaque moment that sends literary-critical minded viewers into enthusiastic character speculation, but it is really anyone's guess as to what we are to make of it. Similarly – are we to believe Hanni and Franz when they declare at the end of *Wildwechsel* that theirs was not 'real love'? Do we believe Effi when, on her death bed, she acknowledges that Instetten was right to behave as he did? Most of us on seeing the films will probably be clear where we stand on such issues – I feel Marlene rejects Petra because she recognises that Petra is incapable of not seeking to control in relationships, that Hanni and Franz truly loved each other, that Effi's final declaration is ironic. But I don't think I could demonstrate these readings from textual evidence – the texts are, in this sense, open.

This tendency towards ambiguous narrative closure is, however, the limit of the films' openness. Elsewhere – in casting, *mise en scène*, composition, etc. – Fassbinder's films can be clearly situated under the rubric of 'left-wing melancholy'.[3] This is admittedly an imprecise term, referring broadly to a view of life that recognises the exploitativeness of capitalist society but is unable to see any means by which a fundamental change in this society can take place. This melancholy is left-wing – and not just a general despair at the human condition – because it sees the specifically (historically determinant) capitalist source and character of misery in contemporary society and observes how the weight of oppression lies on the working class. In its 'melancholy', however, it does not see the working class as the agent of historical change – instead it stresses the working class as the victim of capitalist society and/or as

---

* By effectivity, I do not mean 'effect', which implies a direct impact from the film on to the audience and/or society at large. Rather I want to emphasise the way the films can be taken up, used, made to do political work through discussion, critical debate and so on.

hopelessly complicit in its own oppression. The sexual-political version of this substitutes or adds, for the working class, women and gays. (Left-wing melancholy can also properly show how capitalism and patriarchy deform the lives of the middle classes, men and heterosexuals, even while recognising the advantages and power that these groups have.)

This left-wing melancholy shows itself most obviously in the emphasis on victims in Fassbinder's work. The central figure of many of the films (as of Douglas Sirk's melodramas) is a sufferer – Effi Briest, Franz (*Fox*), Emmi (*Fear Eats the Soul*), Petra von Kant. It is true that the social source of this suffering may be clearly spelt out – marriage, class, racism, in the case of these three films; and even when it is not so clear, there are none the less indications of a source of misery outside the individual character's personality. Men – in the constant reminder of them in the painting in her flat, in Petra's discussion of her marriage with Sidonie, in Karin's taunting of Petra with stories of men she has been with,[4] and, most tellingly, in the way that, following a phone call out of the blue from her husband, she ups and leaves Petra – are indicated as a source of Petra's unhappiness. In *Katzelmacher* – where Jorgos, the *Gastarbeiter*, who suffers most and whose nickname gives the film its title, is not treated as the central figure – male power over women is indicated both in details of the narrative where the men assert physical power over their girl-friends and in contrasting scenes between the men together (where they discuss how to assert their power) and the women together (where, overlit and with romantic piano music playing out of tune over, the discussion is romantic about men). More diffusely, Hanni and Franz in *Wildwechsel* are victims of the hypocrisies of familial sexuality (in the first sequence, with Hanni's mother's reluctant agreement to 'stay on in bed' on Saturday morning, despite what Hanni might think, an agreement then disappointed by the father putting the desires of his pubescent daughter, to be driven to school, before those, now awakened, of his wife), the tattiness of commercial teenage culture, the unpleasant factory conditions in which Franz works, and the incomprehensibility of the law (as Hanni and Franz are caught in the corridor between the courts, while off screen in the court itself their sentences are being decided).

One can show, then, that the social sources of suffering are indicated in the films. The problem is that what we see, what is dwelt on, is the state of being a victim itself. This emphasis is achieved by various means. Andrew Britton discusses the use of fate motifs in *Fox*, with their connotation of an inexorable destiny in which the protagonist is caught. In *Petra von Kant* it is through the use of long takes and prowling camera, particularly in the last third of the film, with Petra lolling on the floor clutching a gin bottle, the camera down there with her, insistently, painfully, for minutes on end. Most characteristic, perhaps, is the use of static compositions that suggest entrapment. Renny Harrigan details some of these in her article on *Effi Briest*; other examples one might cite are – Hanni hopscotching in the bars across the corridor at the end of *Wildwechsel*; Emmi and Ali shot through the doors of the restaurant where they are celebrating their wedding, the walls crowding in on them from both sides of the screen, the shot held on them at the end of a sequence in which the disdain of the waiter has been made quite clear; and, also from *Fear Eats the Soul*, the moment when the Yugoslav woman, who has joined Emmi's cleaners' team and is now relegated below the previously ostracised Emmi, looks straight out to camera through the bannisters (bars) of the stairs. These stylistic procedures may even function to express the victim state of protagonists who might not otherwise be perceived as victims: for example, the group in *Katzelmacher* might not appear victims in the narrative that we see – it is after all they who victimise Jorgos and, within the group, the men are clearly ascendant over the women. However, the shots of them grouped by a handrail in the street that recur throughout the film indicate the group's entrapment in a wider, hinted at mesh of social oppression. These shots are from different distances but always head-on and *static*; the characters are *rigidly* grouped (hence emphasising that they have been shaped as a group), with meaningless slight variations on the grouping from shot to shot; they are *contained* within the frame and around the rail; the harsh light and grainy texture of the image are oppressive. The repetition of the poses within the frame – the women leaning back with their left knee bent, the men sitting with their legs open, also expresses the rigidity of gender roles.

This dwelling on the victim state is not gloating. As Jan Dawson puts it, 'However refined or uncouth the characters ... they are ultimately united by the tremendous compassion with which they are observed'. Yet there is a problem with putting it the way Dawson does. The point-of-view on the characters is compassionate (or, rather more accurately in my view, pitying), but they are characters that Fassbinder has constructed – not singlehandedly, but with his collaborators and drawing on the available modes of representation in the culture. As Dawson puts it, it is as if the films are compassionate for people who already existed and happened to wander in front of the cameras; whereas the films are a construction of the character type 's/he about whom compassion/pity is to be evoked'.

There is what one might call an 'emotionalism' about the representation of these characters, so that the elements of criticism of society become marginalised in favour of the depiction and laying bare of suffering. The repeated use of female protagonists – though it *is* partly to do with the oppression of women and partly because the films are aware enough of sexual politics not to suggest that you can only use women characters when you want to speak of women's, as opposed to class or race, issues – is also to do with, as Fassbinder says in the interview in this book, the idea that 'women can show their emotions more' and hence can be used for greater emotional expressivity; and also with the fact that the suffering woman, woman-as-victim, is a key icon of patriarchal culture. As Susan Brownmiller and Laura Mulvey have argued,[5] one in the context of the culture of rape, the other in relation to the representation of women as sex objects in film, the image of female suffering is, in this culture, a beautiful image. This is in part by virtue of the tender care with which it is painted, sculpted or photographed, but crucially because it places the spectator in a position of power over the represented woman, power that inflates the spectator's ego even if at the same time evoking his* – real and genuine – compassion.⁶

As has been argued, Fassbinder's *mise en scène*, his way of seeing, pins characters down in static takes, traps them between compositional bars. This *mise en scène* both expresses entrapment and distances the spectator, so that we are placed in relation to the films' characters in that position of superiority, albeit caring, that visitors to a zoo have in relation to the caged animals – they are separated from us, and trapped there for our contemplation. There is beauty too in Fassbinder's depiction of victims. Beauty is notoriously hard to define or indicate, and Fassbinder's films are also at times remarkable for their insistent ugliness; yet his choice of performers for central roles is also linked to two traditions of beauty (in film and the surrounding culture). The first, in some of his female protagonists, is the fairly conventional notion of what an attractive woman looks like in Western culture – white, young, even-featured, slim. Hanna Schygulla, featured in fourteen of his films up to and including *Effi Briest* (his sixteenth feature film), is most representative here, especially in *Effi Briest*, where the black and white photography of her in impeccable period clothes recalls that of *Vogue* photographers such as Richard Avedon. The second tradition of beauty is that invoked by various vaguely surrealist-inspired critics and cinéastes, most consistently in the magazine *Midi-Minuit Fantastique*. This is a celebration of the beauty of pain or ugliness in a woman, often with frankly Sadeian implications. Fassbinder does not go so far as *Midi-Minuit*, but there remains a certain fascination with flawed, scarred or 'off' features, especially in characters who are both sympathetic and in other respects attractive, that is, young, elegant, sexy. Eva Mattes' slightly Mongoloid features (*Wildwechsel*), and the flattened face and thin lips of Irm Hermann (Marlene in *Petra von Kant*) are examples here, as is Fassbinder's (as Franz in *Fox*) bashed-in face and squinty eyes. (The films clearly establish these performers as characters who are, respectively, young, elegant, and sexy.) The last example reminds us that it is not only women who are beautiful victims in Fassbinder's films.

It's important to stress here that I am not claiming that Fassbinder's films – and much less Fassbinder the person – are *simply* patriarchal or bourgeois. Rather, the propensity for victims, while it may well be expressive of compassion or pity, is enmeshed in a visual and narrative rhetoric that bespeaks and tends to reinforce a bourgeois patriarchal way of seeing – that is, thinking and feeling about – the oppressed. It also goes hand in hand with some other ideological characteristics of his work.

There is, to begin with, a problem over the films' definitions of class. The problem is partly that there is a preponderance of characters whose class position is marginal – lumpenproletariat (Franz, Emmi, the group in *Katzelmacher*) and even, if the term exists, lumpenbourgeoisie (Petra von

---

* This representation addresses a male spectator, invites him to take up the position described. This does not mean that all men necessarily accept the invitation, nor does it tell us how women place themselves in relation to such representations.

Kant). These are important class positions, not to be ignored, especially in contemporary capitalist society with its commitment to unemployment and its need for a reserve army of labour (cf. Judith Mayne's remarks on Emmi and Ali in her article on *Fear Eats the Soul*) – but they remain marginal, and, by definition, powerless. Moreover, when the films do come to deal with the central structures of capitalist society, they do so in rather odd, or displaced, ways. In *Fox*, Franz is exploited by his bourgeois friends but he is not exploited as a worker – he is exploited as a backer of Eugen's father's printing works. They are able to exploit him because of his working class/lumpen ignorance of capitalist ways (in particular, legalities), but the real relations laid bare are not those of the labour:capital nexus that underpins capitalism.

Another example is *Fear Eats the Soul*. In her article on the film, Judith Mayne argues that it shows how 'the development of capitalist society is marked by relentless and increased domination of the commodity form over all aspects of life'. She points both to aspects of narrative (e.g. Emmi's social reacceptance is represented by the attitude of her grocer, who recognises his need for her as a good customer despite her marrying an Arab; Ali's seeking comfort in the bed of Barbara, the owner of the bar where Emmi and Ali first meet, none the less shows, Mayne suggests, that 'Ali's relationship to Barbara is first and foremost that of customer and proprietor') and also to the way that Emmi and Ali's relationship is constructed through the way others look at them, 'the interplay of objectifying stares' – 'Emmi's relationship to Ali exists for the viewer through the disapproving gazes of her co-workers, neighbours, children and nameless figures in public places. (...) The context of Emmi and Ali's relationship is, in a word, that of reification.' In this perspective, the film's analysis of capitalist society turns out to focus on the market as the key instance of capitalism, not the mode of production. (It also implies that before capitalism much was free that is now commoditised, whereas capitalism replaces with the cash nexus the much worse oppression of feudal obligation.) This has two consequences for Fassbinder's films (though, because of the uncharacteristic delicacy of *Fear Eats the Soul*, the first of these does not apply to it) – the brutalisation of people at the hands of capitalist forces, and the absence of a recognition of labour (by which I understand the production and reproduction[7] of life by human activity) as a potential source of resistance and subversion.

The sense of brutalisation[8] comes through in the insistent crudity and vulgarity of many of the characters (though I would not want to go along with Roger Greenspun's self-revealing comment that 'It is impossible not to sympathise with Eugen's feelings [about Franz's lower-class vulgarities], since [Franz] never consents to use a handkerchief nor, after months of instruction from the accomplished Eugen, learns not to pour the red wine with the fish'). The seedy colour stock of *Wildwechsel* emphasises Hanni's garish taste in clothes and Franz's sallow complexion, while the opening scenes dwell on Hanni's mother picking at her complexion and her father, unshaven and gross in his pyjamas, demanding sex. That this can be seen as brutalisation is suggested by the long tracking shot of the chicken factory where Franz works, in which we see the whole process by which a vividly coloured live animal becomes a soapy white packaged foodstuff. (A brutalisation perspective tends always to stress industrialisation rather than capitalism as the source of workers' misery.) While there is a certain ironic romanticism in the treatment of Hanni and Franz's sex scenes, elsewhere in Fassbinder's work working-class sexuality, especially men's, is seen as immediate and purely genital (without any wider sensuality). This often revolves around discussions of penis size, in which the characters assume that foreign men (e.g. Jorgos) and working-class men (e.g. Franz in Fox) have bigger penises than other men, an assumption the films do nothing to question.

The brutalisation motif in Fassbinder's films obscures the humanity of the class of which the characters are representative, for the depiction could not signal ugliness and disgust if it did not assume a true, unbrutalised humanity somewhere else (in the audience?). Moreover, like the victim emphasis, it implies a model of human society which denies human practice. Fassbinder's films are politically depressing, not only because the characters are defeated but because, since we are to see them as beautiful victims, they don't even try. Hardly anywhere is there a notion of working-class, or women's, or gay, struggle, whether in the form of resistance (not being brutalised by the forces that seek to brutalise) or revolution (overturning those forces). In her article on *Effi Briest*, Renny Harrigan says 'Fassbinder has portrayed a passive, suffering heroine of the upper classes – there weren't many others available if the plot was to be at all realistic' – but this is to ignore precisely the story of women's resistance, of what women have been able to achieve within their subordination, which feminist historians like Sheila Rowbotham have uncovered. It is not that one is calling for a glowing or sentimental model of how 'wonderful' the oppressed are, nor for films to deal only with those active in public politics or to deny the reality of defeat, but rather that it is politically necessary to recognise traditions of resistance and subversion, since they are the root of all other political struggle. To put it another way, the emphasis in Fassbinder's films on people as victims of society and history implies a model of social change that is unable to indicate how people can be actively involved in that process of change – in other words, a model that makes political struggle pointless.

Having said all that, let me now begin to retreat from it in a series of qualifications. First, we are talking about the films, not the man. It is the rhetoric that earns them the indictment of left-wing melancholy; and there is no unproblematic connection between this and Rainer Werner Fassbinder's intentions or political credentials. I stress this not only because I reject any easy equation of a person's thoughts and feelings and the signification of the art s/he is involved in producing, but also because this body of films is widely seen and talked about (relatively) and does address questions of sexual politics. For these reasons, I'd rather have Fassbinder on my side, and I don't want to jeopardise this by calling him names just because I find the films themselves problematic.

Secondly, there are worse things in this world than left-wing melancholy. We are living in a period in which capitalist recession is not visibly being greeted by working-class revolutionary struggle (though there's always plenty of resistance), and which is for artists and intellectuals a retreat from the hopes of May 1968. Moreover, Fassbinder is living in a wealthy country of quite exceptional political repression, which has seen, as in Britain, a disturbing resurgence of fascist politics (with considerable working-class support). On the terrain of sexual politics itself, I acknowledge the force of a line Petra von Kant is given to say: 'People need one another, but haven't learnt how to live together.' This line gets its resonance from what has happened to the sexual political movements – partial and precarious victories at the level of civil rights, equal pay and so on, accompanied by the virtual collapse of the wider aims of liberation in the face of the narrower blandishments of permissiveness.[9] In this context, left-wing melancholy, while it is a fatal political attitude, is also an understandable one.

Thirdly, one of the weaknesses of the films' politics, which the Cant-Britton, Wilson-Sheldon exchanges highlight, is their failure to articulate adequately class and sexual politics. *Fear Eats the Soul* comes nearest to it, but *Effi Briest* and *Fear of Fear* do not explore the class specificities of their female protagonists' oppression, while on the other hand neither *Petra von Kant* nor *Fox* show any awareness that gays are oppressed as gays. Yet, serious as this weakness is, one has to acknowledge that no one else has cracked this particular political nut – neither in films, nor very much in political theory or practice. Fassbinder is better at showing the class dimension (and this is how Ruth McCormick, for instance, appropriates his work, treating the sexual representations as unproblematic metaphors for class relations), but if one compares *Fox* to a film that is very good on gay oppression, *Hunting Scenes from Lower Bavaria* (directed by Peter Fleischmann), one sees very clearly how difficult it is to combine both politics. *Fox* is silent on gay oppression; but *Hunting Scenes from Lower Bavaria*, in terms of class, makes Fassbinder's melancholy view of working-class vulgarity seem positive – not only does *Hunting Scenes* dwell on the coarse sexuality and physical crudeness of its peasant characters, it explicitly compares them to pigs (through a shot of them pursuing the gay protagonist which has the same sickly-sweet music over as was earlier piped into the vast sheds where the pigs are penned). The film is also pretty suspect in its representation of women – yet it remains one of the few films to show quite clearly how male gay oppression works (and does not put the cause of gay suffering in gays' own emotional inadequacy). Set side by side, *Hunting Scenes* and *Fox* show how very hard it is still for anyone to work out the articulations of class and gender/sexuality, respecting both their specificity and their interdependence.

Fourthly, there does seem to be a shift taking place in Fassbinder's work, certainly if his contribution to *Germany in Autumn* is anything to go by. In some ways, this is the most insistently ugly of any of his films that I have seen. Fassbinder as performer wears a shirt that is too tight for, and hence emphasises, his podgy stomach; he is sick, sniffs cocaine, shouts at Armin, bursts into tears; a long-held, low-angle shot of him and Armin at a table emphasises the empty beer bottles and overflowing ashtrays. There is nothing attractive about the situation or the character – yet it is moving in a way different from the compassion displayed/evoked in the earlier films. Partly, no doubt, this is because one recognises Fassbinder as Fassbinder, and this makes the sequence the most unambiguous coming out in his work. Coming out is always a difficult and moving occurrence, and even more so in the context of so 'heavily' political a film as *Germany in Autumn*. What adds to this quality is the sequence's ending, where Armin, who has no political sympathies with the Fassbinder 'character' and has been pretty well abused throughout the sequence, comforts his sobbing friend. It is a moment in which the strength of tenderness – and in the face of squalor – is acknowledged, perhaps for the first time in Fassbinder's work.

Fifthly, it is important to see how some, at any rate, of the problems of Fassbinder's work stem from it being the work of a gay film-maker. This dimension is present not only at the level of subject matter, but also in the elements of camp sensibility in his work. Jack Babuscio's discussion of *Petra von Kant* highlights the way that Fassbinder's much commented on distanciation techniques spring from the emphasis in camp on artifice, theatricality and 'the ironic functions of style'. Much of the rhetoric of Fassbinder's films is camp. As Manny Farber and Patricia Patterson put it: 'All of his appetites (for the outlandish, vulgar and banal in matters of taste, the use of old movie conventions, a no-sweat approach to making movies, moving easily from one media to another, the element of facetiousness and play in terms of style) are those of camp and/or Warhol.'

Camp is an enormously ambiguous phenomenon, ambiguous in its own right as a particular sensibility, and even more so in its relation to the homosexual sub-culture.[10] On the one hand camp is relentlessly trivialising, but on the other its constant play with the vocabulary of straight society (in particular, the excesses of male and female role-playing) sends up that society in a needlingly undermining way. In the last analysis, gay politics and culture are going to have to move beyond the limitations of camp; but we still have to appreciate how central and almost instinctive a feature of the male gay subculture it is, how much many gay men feel at home – for once in their lives – with the camp sensibility. Fassbinder's work is caught up in these ambiguities, and I feel I want to defend his involvement in camp even while acknowledging its problems. The latter include the extreme ambivalence of his/camp's depiction of women, of which Christiane Maybach/Hedwig (Franz's sister in *Fox*) is the clearest instance. Are we to enjoy her strength and commonsense, her warmth, her unabashed vulgarity, or is it her fleshy physicality, her streaked peroxided hair and slobbering lips? – either way she is 'too much', and camp enjoins us to enjoy *both* aspects. Moreover, and this is the real difficulty with camp, the films go into a world where the camp sensibility is barely known or understood, where the dangerous play of ambiguities is read as either gay bad taste, trivialisation and woman-hating or else a depiction of the awfulness of women. None the less, one still has to recognise that it is

Fassbinder's camp that has allowed him to develop the kind of foregrounding techniques which critics have usually preferred to ascribe purely to Brechtianism.

Finally, discussion of camp already leads us to the issue of 'reading', of how these films are appropriated by their audiences. This cannot be construed from an analysis of the films themselves, though the ambiguities of Fassbinder's work are already enough to indicate that his films will be very differently understood by different members of the audience, according to both their structural position in society (class, gender, race, sexual orientation, etc.) and their political orientation. What is clear is that Fassbinder's films are eminently suitable for further debate. This is already evident in the Cant–Britton, Wilson–Sheldon exchanges cited at the beginning of this article, and in the variety of views argued in the various articles I have referred to. At the critical level, Fassbinder's films tend to get discussed in terms of their sexual politics – they put this question on the agenda of critical debate (although a formalist appropriation of his work is possible, as much of the present volume makes clear). At the level of German film culture too, one can see that Fassbinder's films are part of a wider involvement with sexual politics evidenced by such films as *The All-Round Reduced Personality, Hunting Scenes from Lower Bavaria, The Lost Honour of Katharina Blum, Ich liebe dich ich töte dich, The Left-Handed Woman, Armee der Liebenden, Shirin's Wedding* (lesbian films remain a significant absence). It is also my experience that Fassbinder's films often provoke better discussion of sexual political issues than some films that I would argue are more ideologically acceptable. I remember a discussion in a gay liberation group about *Fox*, which centred on the adequacy with which the film dealt with sexual and class politics. The issue of the relationship between these two politics was one that this group was usually reluctant to discuss (many considering it irrelevant), and *Fox* provided the occasion for one of the most productive engagements with the issue that I can remember. At the levels of critical debate, film-making and political use, Fassbinder's work has been *effective* in stimulating debate and thought – even if one does still have to recognise how it is also appropriated by film festivals and art cinema marketing as formalism or apolitical cynicism. That political effectivity – limited though it is – may be far more important than the films' own political despair. In the end, it is not so much what the films say that matters, but rather what people do with what they say.

Articles on Fassbinder cited
Jack Babuscio, 'Camp and the Gay Sensibility' in Richard Dyer (ed): *Gays and Film*, British Film Institute, 1977.
Andrew Britton, 'Foxed', *Gay Left*, no. 3; reprinted in *Jump Cut*, no. 16.
Bob Cant, 'Fassbinder's *Fox*', *Gay Left*, no. 2; reprinted in *Jump Cut*, no. 16.
Jan Dawson, 'Rainer Werner Fassbinder: the prodigal prodigy', *The Listener*, 19 September 1974.
Manny Farber and Patricia Patterson, 'Fassbinder', *Film Comment*, Nov–Dec. 1975.

Roger Greenspun, 'Phantom of Liberty: Thoughts on Fassbinder's *Fist-Right of Freedom*', *Film Comment*, Nov–Dec. 1975.
Renny Harrigan, 'Women Oppressed!', *Jump Cut*, no. 15.
Judith Mayne, 'Fassbinder and Spectatorship', *New German Critique*, no. 12, Fall 1977.
Ruth McCormick, 'Fassbinder and the politics of everyday life – a survey of his films', *Cineaste*, vol. VIII, no. 2.
Caroline Sheldon, 'Lesbians and Film: some thoughts' in *Gays and Film* (op. cit.).
Elizabeth Wilson, 'How Much Is It Worth?', *Red Rag*, no. 10.

Notes

1. This article is based on a limited selection of Fassbinder's films – *Katzelmacher, The Bitter Tears of Petra von Kant, Wildwechsel, Fear Eats the Soul, Effi Briest, Fox* and *Germany in Autumn.*
2. All articles on Fassbinder referred to are listed at the end of this article.
3. The term is associated with Walter Benjamin, who used it to describe the poetry of Erich Kästner and the Neue Sachlichkeit. See 'Left-wing melancholy', *Screen*, vol. 15, no. 2.
4. Here Fassbinder falls into one of the stereotypical scenes in films with lesbian characters – cf., for example, *The Silence* and *The Killing of Sister George.*
5. Susan Brownmiller, *Against Our Will*, Secker and Warburg, London, 1975; Laura Mulvey, 'Visual Pleasure and Narrative Cinema', *Screen*, vol. 16, no. 3.
6. Victims need not be represented beautifully. For example, *Shirin's Wedding*, with its strong sense of the 'otherness' of men rather than women; or *Wanda*, with its thin bedraggled protagonist.
7. By production, I understand the means by which material existence is maintained in society, and by reproduction I understand not only procreation but also the means by which social relations are maintained.
8. I am not sure where the term 'brutalisation' comes from, but it can be located in the kind of social criticism represented by E. A. Shils, Ortega y Gasset and the Orwell of *1984*.
9. See *Gay Left*, no. 2, editorial article, 'Within These Walls'.
10. For further discussion, see Richard Dyer, 'It's being So Camp as Keeps us Going', *Body Politic*, no. 36, Sept. 77; and Andrew Britton, 'For Interpretation – Against Camp', *Gay Left*, no. 7.

Memories of Fassbinder's Television Work

Thomas Thieringer

Fassbinder never stops. Waiting time is production time as far as he is concerned, and everyone, even the distributors, has to keep up with him. It would suit many of them if the energy of this production wonder, who is increasingly a solo film-maker, were to be concentrated on his big-scale project – the filming of the Alfred Döblin novel *Berlin Alexanderplatz*. A mammoth undertaking, like the *Soll und Haben* series which, however, for political reasons fell victim to the 'scissors' in its early planning stages. Both are television projects which will (or that is the intention) provide material for the cinema. But Fassbinder does not seem able to manage this kind of co-production as easily as he does his spontaneous, 'pure' works for the cinema. And so the cinema version of his TV two-parter *Bolwieser* is still not available, even though he announced it at the press screening for the television transmission at the beginning of 1977 and promised it to several festivals. Fassbinder also promised a cinema version totally different from the two-part TV version – completely different visual material was to be used in some sections, and the story was to be 'harder', told in a less epically measured way.

The *Berlin Alexanderplatz* project would provide evidence – the more definitive the better – for speculations about the transformation of the same material. But perhaps Fassbinder, who (to the outside world) always seems able to complete his new projects 'quickly' and 'easily', cannot sustain his patience and interest in the job of rearranging: new projects are more important to him. An indication of this is provided by the filming of some of his theatrical productions – or more precisely the film and television adaptations of his own plays and theatre productions. Fassbinder does not document them, does not try to make his visual approach match his subject, but tries to fit his material to his camera aesthetics. It is noticeable, however, that he sought this tension with existing material primarily in the work he did for the medium of television. It was material based on the ideas of other people – like Volker Schlöndorff in *Rio das Mortes*, Michael Fengler in *Niklashauser Fahrt*, Asta Schein in *Fear of Fear*; or based on plays like his own *Bremer Freiheit*, *Pioniere in Ingolstadt* (after Marie Luise Fleisser), *Nora Helmer* (after Ibsen's *A Doll's House*), *Wildwechsel* (after Franz Xaver Kroetz); or taken from literary texts, as for instance his science-fiction TV film from Daniel F. Galouye's novel *Welt am Draht*, or *Bolwieser* after Oskar Maria Graf.

Nearly all Fassbinder's early television films have been shown in the cinema. The choice of other people's material (the ratio of his own themes to existing texts is approximately 1:2 in his television work, while in his cinema films it is roughly one adaptation to five Fassbinder originals), and the different methods of financing (conditions of production), have not prevented the transfer of his work from one medium to the other. Among the early exceptions are *Niklashauser Fahrt* (co-author and co-director, Michael Fengler), transmitted on 26 May 1970, and the two study sketches (video!) of his plays *Das Kaffeehaus* – the play which saw the culmination and conclusion of his *antiteater* period in Munich – and *Bremer Freiheit*. Although *Niklashauser Fahrt* (1970) was shot as a film (only one print of this Westdeutscher Rundfunk film is available!), it exhibits distinct stylistic parallels with the video sketches (transmitted in January 1971 and November 1973). More emphatically than in his often very statuesque films, he makes use here of parallels, repetitions of similar scenes and visual elements, even whole sequences. Fassbinder's attempt to subject his characters to unchangingly repeated rituals, to show the simultaneous destruction of individual characters (like the poisoner Geesche in *Bremer Freiheit*), was soon recognised as a mannerism because it was imposed on the material from 'outside'. His method of interpretation seemed determined by the simplest and most obvious manipulation of the camera, the greatest number of the lowest common denominator of angles in sequence. An example of the response he got is the reaction to *Das Kaffeehaus* in the 'Critical Opinion' column of the *Süddeutsche Zeitung* of 21 January 1971:

> Money rules them all and the pursuit of the Golden Calf determines everything they do. The burden of the piece, that anyone who is rich and 'aristocratic' can get away with anything and stay on top, is not particularly new. But the style used to revitalise this insight is supposed to be new. Fassbinder and Raben dissect 'coffee house' society in a sterile room in slow motion. There is hardly any action. The only matters of importance are the money-determined relationships of the characters. The camera allows these relationships to develop by maintaining a distance, limiting itself to long and medium shots. But this 'cool' style is really nothing more than a frequently boring device – celebratory theatre. The sugar coating with which Fassbinder covers everything tastes insipid, because he does not make it clear whether he has any interest in the people with whom he is dealing or whom he is manipulating.

The charge of mannerism is strongest in respect of the television work, particularly between 1973 and 1975 when there was a positive 'Fassbinder glut' on television. Fassbinder was repeatedly charged with 'formalistic rubbish', 'effect for effect's sake', 'artificiality'. Although this was passed over when it came to the projection of 'the idea of an idea of an idea' – the adaptation (reminiscent of Howard Hawks' *The Big Sleep*) of Daniel F. Galouye's *Welt am Draht* (transmitted by WDR in autumn 1973) – it seemed that by February 1974 distaste for Fassbinder's 'devices' had reached its height:

> Fassbinder has learnt the trick of turning out quick and effective (?) films, TV plays and theatrical productions. Although much of what he has done

recently can be criticised, he and his team have succeeded time and again in arousing interest in their productions. Fassbinder's directorial ideas [this is a review of *Nora Helmer* in the *Südwest Presse*] are now, since we have become accustomed to his cool style, all too transparent. It is irritating when, as happened in his most recent work as a director, *Nora Helmer*, 'internality' is so patently converted into 'externality' . . . Fassbinder gives us a purely visual illustration of Nora's escape from the gilded cage of her marriage (the doll's house). At first Nora is hidden behind lattice-work and cut glass in her highly decorated, by no means shabby petit bourgeois home. As she withdraws from the life around her, so Fassbinder hides her behind the decor. (This device is used again though less obtrusively in *Bolwieser*.) It is only gradually that the camera comes out of hiding to reveal a wider perspective. At the end, when Nora tells her husband that she has decided to live on her own, there is also a visual dialogue. But even at this point Fassbinder chiefly uses mirrored images (and therefore no direct images!); the characters themselves do not develop in front of the camera. It may be that one could interpret this 'realistically', but it makes Nora's outbreak, her resolve to act, unbelievable. From the outset she is shown to be a self-assured, elegant, calculating woman who, it seems, is only waiting to put her husband in the wrong. The dangers of Fassbinder's 'devices' are evident in his treatment of Margit Carstensen, the actress who plays the title role: he is constantly having to play with lighting effects on her face in order to save her from monotony. Moreover, when all the characters are invested with only *one* attitude, with virtually unvarying tones, any interest in them as individuals rapidly disappears, and that is by no means the same thing as transferring that interest to the problem of social deprivation. . . .

Before *Nora Helmer* (1974) there was the original TV film *Martha*, and a year later *Fear of Fear*. Both of them, the trivial horror version of Fontane's *Effi Briest* (*Martha*) and the 'psycho-thriller' *Fear of Fear*, are more or less 'mannerist' treatments of *the* Fassbinder theme – the destruction that lack of recognition and love can produce, both internally and externally; the exhausting and often futile attempt to experience 'human warmth'. If it was possible to make about *Martha* the weary jibe that 'its form was looking for its content', it was also possible to find in *Fear of Fear* an almost soberly realistic style. In this portrait of a depressive woman, Fassbinder set observation on observation, built up without over-emphasis the motifs of irritation which – as in the earlier *Why Does Herr R Run Amok?* – ultimately led to the highly explicable 'inexplicable' catastrophe. The former observation, that in Fassbinder form is looking for content, can be further documented in these three 'films' where Fassbinder virtually demonstrates how material is altered by its form, in that what he was making were extensive and somewhat stereotyped stylistic exercises on the model of the great 'trivial' Hollywood films (Hitchcock, for example). It is only superficially that Fassbinder has grown out of this phase with his insistence that *I Only Want You to Love Me*, has moved towards the 'popular' realism that he displays in *Wildwechsel*.

In this, his thirtieth film, he tells (once again) the story of a young man who turns to crime through stress and unrequited love. The stimulus was provided by an interview which two sociologists conducted with a murderer condemned to life imprisonment, which very precisely detailed the motivations for fatal, 'surprising', short-circuiting acts of violence. Fassbinder has tried to give an authentic, 'documentary' quality to his film by constantly interpolating sections of the interview which Erika Runge held with a prisoner. In contrast, but also building an authentic atmosphere, are the 'reconstructed' action scenes. Fassbinder tells the story of Peter, a building labourer, subjectively from the perspective of the character's own experience. Peter built his parents a house and received no thanks for it; he married his childhood sweetheart Erika because everyone thought it was a good idea; he provided everything that was good and expensive but found no love – yet the very reason sensitive, unobtrusive Peter took all this on himself was so that he would be accepted and loved. Once again the method is to follow scene with similar scene (of loss). But this method progressively transforms the main character – very accurately portrayed by Vitus Zeplichal – into a pious, stylised scapegoat. He is subjected to greater and greater pressure but, like many of Fassbinder's characters, fails to develop. The result is that here too, unfortunately, while the case history of an 'unmotivated crime' is outwardly explained, our interest in this Fassbinder character quickly dissipates, despite the retrospective documentary scenes. Interest dissipates not because it is redirected by visual mannerisms, but simply because the dramatic development is so transparent that it gives the victim no chance of escape. The dangers inherent in Fassbinder's treatment of his characters are particularly evident in what is otherwise a film of attractive clarity.... (*Südwest Presse*, 26 March 1976.)

And in the *Süddeutsche Zeitung/medium*, August 1977:

R. W. Fassbinder displays his characters in precisely the same way that they exhibit themselves for view in their picture-window homes. Decor is everywhere, art deco as a magnificent disguise. Stranded in the middle of it are the people, the women (and men) deprived of affection and destroying each other, the so very respectable Bolwiesers and Merkls, the Neitharts and the Treubergers – or the 'crazy apes' like Mangst, the railway worker, who don't show their true natures until they are in Nazi uniform. The musical collage, skilfully assembled by Fassbinder's regular composer Peer Raben, also leaves them stranded, washing over their pusillanimous, petty emotional penny-pinching in a flood of variations.

The two-part film from Oskar Maria Graf's novel *Bolwieser*, published in 1931, is Fassbinder's most recent work for television. At first sight it looks like a film-drama-operetta made up of an inventive compilation of all Fassbinder's directorial mannerisms – a bitter *petit bourgeois* tragedy. The last shot of the film is of a broad winter landscape – an image of ultimate loneliness. Over it we hear the alto solo from the fourth movement of

Mahler's Second Symphony – 'Der Mensch liegt in grösster Not!'. It is a kind of transfiguration of the fate of the 'tragic domestic hero', the objectivisation of a 'private mental confusion'; for in this film (after Graf) Fassbinder is also, alongside the personal interest in the characters, telling the story of an unpolitical *petit bourgeoisie*, disoriented and denying the existence of everything which is not supposed to exist or which disturbs its short-term self-interest, a *petit bourgeoisie* which, deeply insecure, seeks refuge in the immediate satisfaction of its desires, and in getting drunk, and which allows itself to be dominated by ruthless jobbers and the prophets of the new political salvation. In the godforsaken flight to the 'safety' of an empty idyll nobody realises what is really happening. People cling to keeping up appearances, and deliver themselves up to destruction – private catastrophe is as inevitable as that which befalls society. Perhaps in none of Fassbinder's previous films has there been so much aural mood painting; in no previous film has the view of the thoroughly divided, tragi-comic action been so purposefully split up by glass, veils and soft focus, or multiplied and shattered by reflections – magnifying glasses with which Fassbinder accentuates (though does not coarsen) the gestures of dangerous helplessness, of brutal subjugation, with which he blows up the ignorant, fatal philistinism of these 'guiltless' people into something monstrous, and under which he dissects the ingrained lies of the way they live. But Fassbinder is not condemning these people, in spite of all the hypocrisy with which he invests them. On this occasion, with singular patience and great aesthetic subtlety, he has succeeded in displaying their inner reality, turned outwards, and in bringing his audience within the magnetic field of an individual alien to them and a society incapable of humanity. The narrative sweep, adapted to television, seems here an ideal match for Fassbinder's 'style'. With *Bolwieser*, Fassbinder has managed (for the first time since *Chinese Roulette*) to produce an exciting 'truth game' – a great, measured and exciting television ... film.

Translated by Barrie Ellis-Jones

Eight Hours are not a Day

Manuel Alvarado

'We had started that week talking about the novels of working-class life ... We'd been discussing why life in a working-class home is so described, (but) the work itself hardly ever.'
      Raymond Williams (from the essay *The Teaching Relationship: Both Sides of the Wall*, in *Education for Democracy*, edited by David Rubinstein and Colin Stoneman, Penguin 1970).

In 1972, having produced thirteen feature films in three years, Fassbinder was commissioned by WDR (Westdeutscher Rundfunk, one of the stations of the first German TV channel, the ARD) to make a family series. This was the first time that he had worked directly for a TV company, and the series he was to produce – *Acht Stunden sind kein Tag (Eight Hours are not a Day)* – marked a new development in his work, in that he was aiming to attract a mass audience. At the time it certainly seemed strange that a director who had gained some critical attention for a group of highly stylised aesthetic 'art house' films should become involved in the production of a 'family series', a genre particularly despised by critics yet attracting the highest TV audience ratings.

It is not entirely clear whether the term 'family series' denotes that the series is about families, watched by families, or both. Whichever the case, it will be useful to compare *Eight Hours are not a Day* with its closest British counterpart *Coronation Street*, as the similarities and differences are both interesting and illuminating. I shall briefly indicate some of the more obvious points of comparison, but an exhaustive analysis would clearly require extensive research work.

Coronation Street and *Eight Hours are not a Day* fulfil both interpretations of the term 'family series': they are about families, and are (were) screened at peak family viewing times. More significantly, they are 'about' working-class families. As such, they make an important contribution to the generation of dominant working-class images, characters and situations, which, though not unique to TV, are remarkably rare in our middle-class dominated media. (The fact that both series were created by middle-class producers, though undoubtedly important, will not be my direct concern here.)

The important initial questions to ask are: *how* are the working class depicted in *Coronation Street*, and how different is their presentation in *Eight Hours are not a Day*? The location of the action in *Coronation Street* is mainly the enclosed world of the street itself. The community contains no children and its members are rarely seen at work. In fact, the work that we do see going on could be loosely described as petit-bourgeois: shopkeeping, the running of a public house, Len Fairclough (a self-employed builder) banging a nail into a wall. The 'world' of *Coronation Street* (and we are encouraged to think of it as a microcosm of the world, a representative sample; witness, for example, the title sequence, showing the street as just one among many thousands of similar streets) is safe, secure, 'a-political', a place where nothing more than petty bickering, gossip and the occasional feud is allowed to disturb the nature and structure of the characters' lives. They are essentially locked into, and resigned to, their position and role in society. The families, apparently lacking children, relatives and employment, lead insular, isolated and static lives. Their dynamic potential for any action that might transform their own or anyone else's existence is entirely absent. By describing *Coronation Street* in this way I am not simply arguing that the series is 'unrealistic', but that the structured absences are deliberate and significant. Their significance lies in the negative and paralysed portrayal of the working class, a portrayal that is reinforced by the occasional 'social realist' TV documentary, where the images depict a sad and acquiescent group of people.

The 'world' of *Eight Hours are not a Day* is strikingly different. Clearly the constraints under which the series was produced are not the same as those in force at Granada, where *Coronation Street* is made. Westdeutscher Rundfunk provided a fairly large amount of money to produce a series of predetermined length; originally there existed the possibility of making eight long episodes, but eventually only five were made.

Eight Hours are not a Day set out to present a total view of workers' lives and problems: the characters are seen in a number of locations – home, friends' homes, bars, clubs, the factory floor and the factory yard. Furthermore, the intention was explicitly to contradict the conventional 'social realist' image of the worker, because however sincere such sympathy with workers as betrayed members of society might be, to attach such a representation to people themselves as something accurate and inescapable is clearly wrong. The project of *Eight Hours are not a Day* was therefore not to present a 'realistic' portrayal of workers' living conditions but instead to create positive images to demonstrate the possibility of living within those conditions and, more importantly, of changing them. Thus we see Jochen and his mates at work, experiencing all the problems of work (working conditions, pressure of output, bonus schemes, wages), and in bars discussing these problems. All of this forms a context for Jochen's domestic life. Social relationships within a family are shown through the ways they deal with and reflect on the problems they experience at a domestic level: the rent they pay for their flat, the establishment of a kindergarten, the use of the bathroom. While disagreements are shown, what is clearly indicated is a solidarity among the different inter-related groups: for instance, the unity of the workers in their negotiations with the management, the exchange of flats in episode 5, the help provided for the elderly couple Oma and Gregor in episode 2, Oma 'protecting' Monika in episode 5. In general, members of the working class are depicted positively as beginning to control, organise and change their apparent destiny.

Interestingly, the isolated, weak and potentially alienated people in the series are the representatives of the ruling class: the factory boss, remote in his 'op-art' office, the 'smooth' confidence trickster in episode 5. It is worth pointing out that the working class presented is not the 'lumpen proletariat' but the labour 'aristocracy' (skilled tool makers), but the important aspect is that they are treated as *subjects* of the narrative and not as *objects* (that is, capable of action, and not the passive recipients of other people's actions). Fassbinder clearly determined that it was the turn of the ruling class to be treated as objects. This is probably an oversimplification of the role of the boss, but in an interview Fassbinder did state explicitly that his aims were 'to make things which are dangerous to the so-called ruling class'.

Although the subject's political implications are foregrounded, Fassbinder was very concerned about the popularity of the series. Well aware of the fact that a large proportion of the public tend to evade serious political discussion, he realised that the series had to have entertainment value to ensure that it would be transmitted, let alone be successful in audience ratings. This is the classic dilemma that anyone who tries to make political programmes within a capitalist system has to confront. In the case of *Eight Hours are not a Day,* it results in a number of interesting features. For instance, there is a notable absence of institutions like trade unions and political parties, which means that their importance and influence in working-class life is ignored. At the time, Fassbinder received heavy criticism for this omission, but he claimed that their inclusion would have reduced the popular appeal of the programmes. In fact he did intend to introduce such organisations in episodes 6-8, which was perhaps one of the reasons that WDR decided not to continue the series. If that was the case, it would clearly reinforce Fassbinder's argument.

The intention was first to 'capture' an audience by entertaining them, and only then to encourage the viewers to reflect on the problems raised. Thus the first episode begins with a number of amusing domestic situations, which by episode 5 have largely (but significantly not totally) been displaced by a concentration on problems related to the work situation. As all the characters, throughout the series, have been changing and developing their personal relationships, so have they also been developing and changing their situations at work. Both processes involve their development of a clearer and better understanding of the world.

Just as Fassbinder places the potential for this analysis and change with the workers, thus subverting the dominant media image of the working class, so he also places it with the representatives of two other oppressed groups in our society: women and old people. Marion's role in *Eight Hours are not a Day* is crucial because she is seen to be a central agent in the development of the workers' consciousness. She is a middle-class secretary who leaves her stereotypically handsome, middle-class boyfriend for a not conventionally handsome factory worker, much against her mother's wishes. She becomes part of the workers' milieu (as eventually does her office girlfriend), and at times even sits in the controlling position at the head of the table. It is important that in order to present a positive image of women a conventionally beautiful woman be seen to offer an intelligent, political critique of the workers' actions. Similarly, Oma and Gregor are presented as operating in a positive and dynamic way (for instance, the opening of the kindergarten), and are shown to have a warm *sexual* relationship. This counters the traditional media depictions of old people as either comic caricatures (e.g. Clive Dunn in British TV programmes) or drab, helpless figures in 'social realist' documentaries. The warm humour of the scenes with Oma and Gregor depends on the situational comedy of family life – a life of which they are very much a part – and never works at the expense of them or old people in general. A fourth area of oppression – racial prejudice – is confronted in the workers' discussions about the position of *Gastarbeiter* (immigrant workers) in the factory, but this is not of such central concern in this particular series.

Although the *content* of *Eight Hours are not a Day* is concerned with recognising the political nature of all aspects of life, the *form* of the series clearly does not have the status of radical film-making of the type represented by a director like Godard. In Godard's later films, narrative and stylistic breaks and ruptures are designed to interrogate and 'deconstruct' bourgeois conventions of representation. Godard foregrounds the production of the film itself in an attempt to force the audience to positively confront, reflect and act upon the political problems presented.

Fassbinder, on the other hand, works in a melodramatic tradition, deriving directly from films like those of Douglas Sirk. But the very fact that he adopts an obviously self-conscious, aesthetically beautiful style and applies it to the presentation of working-class problems foregrounds the artificiality of all construction; the method is very different from Godard's 'deconstruction' tactics, but very useful given Fassbinder's desire to achieve popular appeal.

A great deal of work needs to be carried out on the analysis of Fassbinder's style; I will simply indicate some of the techniques he adopts. He employs very complicated camera movement: there is frequent tracking, panning, craning and sudden zooming of the camera, sometimes in combination within a single shot. The almost constant movement is coupled with the highly organised framing of each shot to produce an obviously artificial, self-conscious mode of representation. For example, characters are often shot with an out-of-focus object on the table in front of them, or 'framed' by plants, doorways, etc. The women, in particular, often have carnations or other flowers in front or to one side of them, creating stereotypical 'romantic' images. It is in relation to this that the scene in the bar in episode 5 shows Marion with the workers' half-empty beer glasses in front of her to such significant effect. Camera positioning makes the factory boss appear dominated by the expensive objects that surround him. Similarly, every time a worker walks across the factory floor the camera tracks alongside him, but on the other side of the machines that he is walking past, so that he is continually first isolated and then hidden by the camera movement. This apparent domination of man by machine is eventually reversed in the scene in episode 5 where (to a background of music) the workers are shown controlling the machinery and happy to be in that position of control – what must be the most lyrical and yet seemingly bizarre sequence in the whole series.

One question that must be raised in the context of *Eight Hours are not a Day* is: how radical can a popular film be? To what extent has Fassbinder managed to create a potentially radical, popular film practice? It's worth pointing out now that the series was produced by a group of media workers, and that it is therefore not linked to a specific struggle or situation. Also that it is not concerned with interrogating capitalist methods of production. What the series does attempt to do is to offer a critique of a bourgeois culture that is class-ridden, sexist, racist and age-ist. *Eight Hours are not a Day* represents an interesting attempt to create a popular TV series that reformulates the modes of representing that culture through its media productions.

Afterword

Three years after writing the foregoing (its brevity due both to the nature of the commission and to the fact that it had only been possible to see two of the five programmes, and those in very unfavourable conditions) I finally managed to see all the episodes. I am now fairly certain – despite certain misgivings – that this particular TV series represents Fassbinder's most interesting and important work, and demands much more detailed analysis. However, given the difficulty of viewing the programmes outside West Germany, I would like here to make some further observations about this series in relation to British television and to explain what I think is its importance. My observations fall into two distinct sections.

1

In the original essay I compared *Eight Hours are not a Day* with *Coronation Street*, about which I made a few brief and rather schematic points. This time I want to refer to one specific period in the history of *Coronation Street's* production – in 1974 when Susi Hush was the producer. Her appointment was heralded as indicating that the series would undergo a shift in both focus and direction. A known 'progressive' in the TV world, she would, it was thought, attempt to effect a change in the concerns of the series by introducing situations which would reflect a certain social consciousness – thereby potentially shifting the programme more into line with a family series like *Eight Hours are not a Day*. In fact, more contemporary and 'important' issues did appear, such as drugs, Northern Ireland, racial minorities. Other things changed too: episodes were allowed to have longer scenes (in one room) and there was some use of more self-conscious camera angles (sometimes making direct filmic references). However, this potential 'politicisation' of the series was completely negated in a number of ways, the most obvious being that these important issues were 'introduced' but not 'confronted'.

A brief example will explain. In one episode, a young soldier arrives at the local pub to inform one of the characters that her son has been killed in Northern Ireland. It is then revealed that he died in a car accident – no reference at all is made to the war in Northern Ireland. In addition, the messenger is black, but that too is a narratively unremarked fact. I would argue that this was typical of the way Susi Hush 'modernised' the series, which ironically highlighted the remoteness of the world depicted – although I don't think that this gap exposed the contradictions of representation which would have enabled the viewer to produce an alternative, radical reading of the programme.

But even if the subject matter of the series at this period had been in contradiction with the dominant ideologies of British society (which it certainly wasn't), the extent to which the series could be deemed either progressive or conservative/reactionary would also depend, as Colin McArthur has pointed out, on 'the extent to which its formal strategies mark a departure from the dominant film or television discourses of that society'. And the series in no way departed technically from these discourses even if they were not the same ones normally used in *Coronation Street*. Critically, the response to this period of the programme's history was that it was boring. (A response I share, though for very different reasons. I find it interesting that many critics equate social consciousness with boredom when it occasionally surfaces in a primarily 'entertainment' programme – it is considered inappropriate. And yet many such reviewers also accuse the television companies of producing 'mindless' entertainment.) Granada Television also considered this period unsuccessful (audience ratings fell) and Susi Hush left, whereupon *Coronation Street* reverted to its more traditional concerns and modes.

2

The second area I want to take a little further concerns the questions I posed at the end of the original essay. How radical can a popular film be, and to what extent has Fassbinder managed to create a potentially radical, popular film practice? I will do so by referring to the debate between Colin MacCabe and Colin McArthur around the problem of 'realism' and the possibility of the 'classic realist text' being 'progressive' or 'revolutionary'.*

---

* See C. MacCabe, 'Realism and the Cinema: Notes on some Brechtian theses', *Screen*, vol. 15, no. 2; C. McArthur, 'Days of Hope', *Screen*, vol. 16, no. 4; C. MacCabe, 'Days of Hope – A Response to Colin McArthur', *Screen*, vol. 17, no. 1; C. MacCabe, 'Principles of Realism and Pleasure', *Screen*, vol. 17, no. 3; C. McArthur, *Television and History*, British Film Institute, 1978.

MacCabe summarises his position on realism as follows:

> While traditional debates about realism have centred on content and the ability to reflect reality, classic realism should be considered as centrally defined by a certain formal organisation of discourses whereby the narrative discourse is placed in a situation of dominance with regard to the other discourses of the text. The narrative discourse does not just dispose the other discourses, it compares them with the truth or falsity transparently available through its own operations. The political question of such a realism is then whether this dominant discourse is in conflict with the predominant ideological discourses of the time. I argued further, however, that this formal organisation of discourses is fundamentally compromised by the relationship between reader and text on which it depends. The simple access to truth which is guaranteed by the meta-discourse depends on a repression of its own operations and this repression confers an imaginary unity of position on the reader from which the other discourses in the film can be read....
>
> In order to fracture this unity it would be necessary to pose the problem of the conditions of representation; it would be necessary to interrogate the reality of the constitutional tradition which allows films like *Days of Hope* to be shown on television. To pose these problems would also and immediately pose the problems of the lessons of what happened then for the situation today – the transparent immediacy of the film would be broken by analysis. Only thus could the position of the viewer be fractured, and with no obvious assigned position he or she would have to work on the material. It could be objected, at once, that such a film would have a much smaller audience than *Days of Hope* managed to attract.

This last point was crucial to the debate. The sort of text MacCabe was arguing for was what he termed 'revolutionary' and which was exemplified in films such as Brecht's *Kuhle Wampe*, Godard's *Deux ou Trois Choses que je sais d'elle* and *Tout va bien*, and Oshima's *Death by Hanging*. Implicitly, McArthur's position is that because of the smallness of the potential audience for such texts (which he queries as being utopian), however much he might agree with MacCabe, a 'progressive' realist text such as *Days of Hope* might be 'a more appropriate agitational weapon'. MacCabe had previously defined the progressive realist text as follows:

> There is, however, a level of contradiction into which the classic realist text can enter. This is the contradiction between the dominant discourse of the text and the dominant ideological discourses of the time. Thus a classic realist text in which a strike is represented as a just struggle in which oppressed workers attempt to gain some of their rightful wealth would be in contradiction with certain contemporary ideological discourses and as such might be classified as *progressive*.

Thus McArthur argues that a programme like *Days of Hope* is significantly different from other British television programmes both at the level of its subject matter and at the formal level. But the major point is that *Days of Hope* was watched by a great many people whereas the 'revolutionary' text is entirely absent from the British television screen. The other important point argued by McArthur is that a programme like *Days of Hope* has to be defended by the left when it is attacked (on fairly stupid grounds) from the right.

I have quoted at length from this debate because I suspect that *Eight Hours are not a Day* (along with the rather different but, in my opinion, single most interesting British television programme, the adaptation of the 7:84 Theatre Company's play *The Cheviot, The Stag and the Black, Black Oil*) could be described as occupying a third position which is neither 'progressive' nor exactly 'revolutionary', and which I shall call 'radical'. This term needs precise definition; for the moment I would argue that it goes some way to fulfilling some of the requirements MacCabe would demand for a 'revolutionary' text (with which I am in agreement) while being capable of achieving a mass popular appeal. I would suggest that the way in which *Eight Hours are not a Day* achieves this textually (we know as fact that the series achieved a mass popular audience) is through two important dislocations – one in the recorded phonetic sound track and one in the moving photographic image (to adopt Christian Metz's terminology in 'Methodological Propositions for the Analysis of Film', *Screen*, vol. 14, no. 1/2, 1973).

The first dislocation is achieved by Fassbinder's use of a deliberately mannered, almost expressionistic camera style, which is strikingly at odds with the normal mode of filming proletarian situations. This provides a constant and complex interaction between the *what* and the *how* of the representation offered. This dislocation is reinforced by the second: the fact that the workers and their families speak in *Hochdeutsch* (High German) as opposed to the proletarian dialect which would have been 'realistic'. MacCabe writes of the concept of 'realism' and its relation to the 'real': 'Realism is no longer a question of an exterior reality nor of the relation of reader to text, but one of the ways in which these two interact. The film-maker must draw the viewer's attention to his or her relation to the screen in order to make him or her "realise" the social relations that are being portrayed.'

How successful *Eight Hours are not a Day* is in these terms I cannot say, particularly on the basis of the limited viewing that has been possible; but I would argue that a very important attempt has been made by Fassbinder in this series to work towards that end. To return to my original questions concerning the possibility of a radical film/TV practice, I would like to suggest that the third form of classic realistic text into which Fassbinder's series falls be termed the 'radical realist text'. 'Radical' for two reasons. First, within the terms of the debate referred to I would argue that such a series was radical because it did not simply 'improve' (i.e. redress the balance of) certain representations of the world, as progressive texts do; nor is it a revolutionary text as defined by MacCabe: '... which rather than the simple subversion of the subject or the representation of different (and *correct*) identities, would consist of the displacement of the subject within ideology – a different constitution of the subject.' Secondly, 'radical' because within the context of television a series does not *need* to operate the levels of narrative closure as is currently the case, and *Eight Hours are not a Day* in part represents some progress towards recognising that fact.

Unfortunately, I suspect that there is another, contradictory and ironic, reason for using the term 'radical' which relates to Fassbinder's personal political position. In the context of his total output so far, *Eight Hours are not a Day*, in my opinion, represents his most important and sustained work – the political potential of the early work is finally realised in its most coherently articulated and developed form. However, Fassbinder's subsequent work clearly demonstrates an increasing cynicism and opportunism that makes the achievement of *Eight Hours are not a Day* all the more striking. It is this fact which suggests the greater value of locating the series within the generic context of the *Arbeiterfilm* ('worker film') produced by West German television rather than within the auteurist context of *Fassbinder*. By thus shifting the focus of critical attention one begins to wonder if Fassbinder, while clearly being a 'skilful' film-maker, doesn't simply adopt an eclectic and nihilistic position which allows him, on occasion, to appear 'radical' – and that, of course, is to relegate his position to that of 'radical chic'.

Fassbinder, Form and Syntax

Tony Rayns

1

The formal and syntactic determinants in force in Fassbinder's early films have little or nothing to do with Hollywood models. The rudimentary technique in films like *Love is Colder than Death*, *Katzelmacher* and *Gods of the Plague* certainly belies an assertive stance, a desire to create 'strong' meanings and effects. This stance could be construed as a challenge to Hollywood's classical 'affirmative discourse', but the stylistic strategies that support it have as little to do with Hollywood film grammar as those in Warhol/Morrissey's moral homilies on life amongst the hookers and junkies of the Village. There are three direct inputs into the style of early *anti-teater* films: Straub, the *anti-teater* theatre practice, and the French 'new wave' in general and certain Godard films in particular. From Straub came the sense that a little can be enough, together with a fondness for attenuation, compression and ellipsis. From the theatre work came not only an acting style but an entire *mise en scène* comprising exercises in 'kinesics', the science of placement and gesture. From Godard and his contemporaries came a kind of informal formalism, plus a preference for locations and natural source lighting. All three inputs are virtually antithetical to Hollywood norms.

2

But the single most decisive factor determining the form and character of the early films was finance. Everything about the way the films were conceived and shot reflects the startling poverty of means at the film-makers' disposal. Long, uninterrupted master takes without cutaways, inserts or reverse-field cuts are not only aesthetically (politically?) different from Hollywood's classical syntax, but also significantly cheaper to shoot.

3

The stylistic evolution in Fassbinder's work is relatable to his increasingly frequent collaborations with the cinematographer Michael Ballhaus, begun in *Whity* and *Beware of a Holy Whore* (which respectively parallel the ebullient fatalism of *Une femme est une femme* and the ironic self-consciousness of *Le mépris*). This evolution is characterised by its determination to meet Hollywood discourse, in all its 'affirmative' expansiveness and syntactic density, on its own terms. The films begin to use social, cultural and cinematic conventions for their distinctiveness rather than their banality, a change reflected in a film syntax as alert to details as to generalised views. However, Ballhaus/Fassbinder's aim is to *equal* Hollywood, not to emulate it. In the early 70s, Fassbinder worked with Ballhaus only on those of his projects that were furthest removed from naturalism: *Petra von Kant*, *Martha*, *Welt am Draht* and parts of *Effi Briest*. Ballhaus' predilection for moving camerawork was allowed ever freer rein until the point was reached (in *Chinese Roulette*) where continuously mobile camerawork became a key semantic factor, outweighing dialogue and performances. This kind of style shading into visual rhetoric has clear affinities with certain Hollywood 'fringe' figures (Ophuls, von Sternberg), but none with classical Hollywood syntax. Now that Fassbinder has broken with Ballhaus, and begun photographing his own films, it seems probable that a new visual strategy will emerge.

4

The fact that *Effi Briest* stands as a summation of Fassbinder's work up to 1974 points to the continuities that exist between the *anti-teater* films and the post-1971 films. The claustrophobic long takes of the gangster films feed into the more lavish stylistic *anomie* of *Petra von Kant*. The tableau compositions of *Katzelmacher* feed into the reaction-shots in *Fear Eats the Soul* and the elegantly oppressive stases of *Effi Briest*. The 'camp' theatricality of *Whity* feeds into the enervated chic of *Martha*. *Effi Briest* itself remains Fassbinder's most densely constructed text, demanding a more intensive act of reading from the viewer than any of the other films. Its most 'radical' anti-Hollywood gesture is its continual reference back to the material existence of Fontane's novel, through inter-titles, narration and a *mise en scène* drained of action and even incident. The artifice is foregrounded throughout both formally (the stylised sequence-shots) and syntactically (the emphatic fades to white), and the resulting identification of social oppression with formal closure and stasis effectively synthesises the mood of the early films with the structural dynamics and volatility of the later ones.

5

What Fassbinder sensed in Sirk, Walsh and a few other preferred Hollywood directors was their ironic perspective on much of their material, which he perceived as intimations of *impossibility* vis-à-vis the subject. This perception led him to re-examine the option of using genre-forms, abandoned after *Whity* and the gangster films. His subsequent melodramas, from *The Merchant of Four Seasons* and *Fear Eats the Soul* to *Fox*, still owed little to Hollywood models in the event: their genre was one of his own devising, with scant regard for the plausibility of its devices and conventions (the Foreign Legion motif in *Merchant*; the entire plot of *Fox*). In other words, Fassbinder made 'impossibility' a subject in itself, thereby denying the very possibilities of subversion that he found in Sirk and others. It was doubtless an awareness of this gap between Hollywood practice and his own practice that led Fassbinder into the self-parodying manias of *Satan's Brew*, just as the steadfast deviation from Hollywood models pushed him inexorably in the direction of the European 'art film' and *Despair*.

6
In later films, Fassbinder does occasionally play on viewer recognition of devices from classical Hollywood discourse. Such instances almost invariably occur only in his films for TV: one example would be the visually distorted subjective shots in *Fear of Fear*, which play on audience nostalgia for a style that has vanished even from American cinema. More often, though, his shot compositions and editing syntax resemble comic-strips more than existing films: the heightened simplicity of character groupings, poses and colour co-ordinations, the 'brick-by-brick' shot sequences that fragment simple actions and reactions into distinct segments, both formal devices which evoke the panel structure of comic-strip graphics.

7
The question that must dominate discussion of Fassbinder's existing films is this: is it enough to *replace* Hollywood forms and syntax with idiosyncratic, unpredictable styles of one's own if one wishes to create a cinema that is critical and at the same time popular? Or is it necessary to *transform* Hollywood forms and syntax?

Five Interviews with Fassbinder

Christian Braad Thomsen

1: Berlin 1971/Venice 1972

Before you began making films, you wrote and produced plays in the theatre – or rather the 'anti-theatre', as you called it. Why did you gradually turn to cinema?

In the very beginning, I actually made two short films. I *then* went into the theatre. It was theatre, not anti-theatre. 'Anti-theatre' was just the name we gave it, in the same way that another stage might be called the 'Schiller Theatre'. I have learned a lot in the theatre, about how to work with actors and how to tell a story in a new way. Incidentally, I'm a trained actor myself: it's the only training I've ever really had. Everything else, I've had to teach myself. I wanted to make films from the start, but it was much easier to begin in the theatre. And it has paid off: when I *did* start making films, my previous work in the theatre made it much easier to get credit. The success of my early films, the very fact that they were invited to festivals and that sort of thing, had something to do with theatre enjoying more respect than film in Germany. You'd hear, 'Well, yes, he makes films – but he's done plays too, so the guy must have something'.

Most of your films are influenced by American gangster movies and melodramas, although they are quite different from them. What attracts you in genre films by directors like Raoul Walsh and Douglas Sirk?

It's not easy to explain. Those films tell their stories simply, straightforwardly, suspensefully. Before I made *Whity*, I looked at several Raoul Walsh films, especially at *Band of Angels* (1957, with Clark Gable, Yvonne de Carlo and Sidney Poitier), which is one of the loveliest films I've ever seen. A white farmer dies, leaving behind the daughter he's had by a black woman. The girl looks completely white, but as soon as the old man is dead she is sold, to help clear his debts. Clark Gable plays the slave trader who buys her: he knows she is a negro and she knows he is a slave trader. Then the Civil War starts. Sidney Poitier plays the slave trader's faithful servant and, even though he is fighting on the other side, he helps his master to flee with the girl. So everything works out fine. Or does it? A good director can contrive a happy ending that leaves you dissatisfied. You know that something is wrong – it just can't end that way.

American cinema is the only one I can take really seriously, because it's the only one that has really reached an audience. German cinema used to do so, before 1933, and of course there are individual directors in other countries who are in touch with their audiences. But American cinema has generally had the happiest relationship with its audience, and that is because it doesn't try to be 'art'. Its narrative style is not so complicated or artificial. Well, of course it's artificial, but not 'artistic'.

But your films are 'artistic'.

Yes, but that's because a European doesn't have the same naiveté as a Hollywood director. We have no choice but to consider very carefully what to produce and how to produce it. But I am sure that one day I will succeed in telling naive stories. I am constantly trying to do that, although it's very hard. American directors can work from the idea that the USA is the land of freedom and justice ... I find that very beautiful. But I've never tried to copy a Hollywood film in the way the Italians have. Our films have been based on our *understanding* of the American cinema, or at least, they were at the beginning.

When you say that the only films you can take seriously are those that reach an audience, how does that leave you feeling about your own films, which haven't had much of an audience so far?

That isn't my fault. It's due to a specific economic situation in Germany today. When that situation is changed, my films will have an audience. They show third-rate stuff in German cinemas. The cinema is a business, and it's easier to sell poor films. But I'm sure this will change. It has already changed in France: Chabrol now makes films for a big audience, but he, too, started out making them for a small group. It took him twelve years to reach a wider audience.

Unlike many other so-called 'radical' directors, you give your films a very direct emotional appeal – which might win the public over.

Feelings are very important to me, but feelings are being exploited by the film industry today, and that is something I hate. I am against speculation in feelings.

Perhaps your ambivalent attitude to emotions finds its way into your films when you show an emotionally charged scene but hold the shot so long and move the camera so slowly that you produce a kind of alienation?

Yes, stylistically it is a kind of alienation. I approach the subject of a scene like this: when the scene lasts a long time, when it's drawn out, then the audience can really see what is happening between the characters involved. If I started cutting within a scene like that, then no one would see what it was all about.

So you don't consider these drawn-out scenes as parodies of American genre films?

No, not at all. Some critics think that I use references to American genre films in an ironic way, and of course I can understand how they get that idea and I must accept it. To me, though, it isn't like that. The main difference between American films and mine is that the American cinema is not contemplative – and I, too, would like to achieve a style that unfolds freely, without all these reflections.

I normally divide my films into two groups. There are the bourgeois films, which are all set in a fairly well defined bourgeois environment, and then there are the cinema-films, which are set in typical film environments and contain action of the sort you usually see in cinemas. The first group mirrors quite specific bourgeois mechanisms, and the second group is inspired by films of various genres.

But the genre films, too, are played out in bourgeois surroundings.

Yes, the gangster environment is a bourgeois setting so to speak turned on its head, with the same old bourgeois ideals instead of alternative ideals. My gangsters are victims of the bourgeoisie, not rebels. If they were rebels, they would have to do something else. Since they aren't, they do fundamentally the same things as capitalists do in bourgeois society, except that they do them as criminals. It really makes no difference whether a character in my films is a gangster or a lousy capitalist: the gangster's goals are just as bourgeois as the capitalist's. Perhaps this is another difference between my films and American films, where gangsters sometimes really are outsiders. My gangsters and small-time thieves are actually integrated into society.

2: Berlin 1973

Most of your films see the world through the eyes of a man. But since you've started working with the actress Margit Carstensen, you've centred several projects on a female protagonist: the stage and TV productions of Bremen Freedom, *and the TV adaptation of Ibsen's* A Doll's House. *To start with* Petra von Kant, *though: why does the servant Marlene walk out at the end, when Petra offers her freedom and equality?*

Because the servant accepts her own repression and exploitation, and is therefore afraid of the freedom she is offered. What goes with freedom is the responsibility of having to think about your own existence, and that is something that she has never had to do; she has always simply followed orders, and never had to make her own decisions. When she finally leaves Petra, she is not, I think, heading for freedom but going in search of another slave-existence. Many people seem to have the impression that she is finally freeing herself, but I don't think that at all. It would be wildly optimistic, even utopian, to imagine that someone who has done and thought nothing for thirty years except what others have thought for her would all of a sudden choose freedom.

What was the thrust of your interpretation of A Doll's House *for* TV?

There, too, I made it quite clear that I didn't see it as a question of a woman's emancipation, which is the way the play is conventionally read. All the people in the play, including Nora, need to gain their freedom; Nora is not someone who finally 'sees the light'. At the end, she's as stupid as she always was, and the struggle between her and Helmer seems to me to be a fight over petty details. It's not a serious effort to find a plausible way of living together. On the contrary, it's a struggle to win on certain points, which is something I find very cheap, but also very realistic. I haven't been able to find a shred of evidence in Ibsen's text for taking Nora as an advocate of women's liberation.

I'm often irritated by all the talk about women's liberation. The world isn't a case of women against men, but of poor against rich, of repressed against repressors. And there are just as many repressed men as there are repressed women.

Did you change Ibsen's text?

We didn't change anything, but we eliminated quite a lot. Our Nora, for example, doesn't leave at the end. She stays. You can find the kind of problem that Nora and Helmer had in ten thousand other marriages, and the wife doesn't usually leave – where would she go? People usually try to manage one way or another, which is really even more appalling. You can criticise a set-up like that rather than simply saying a person is free to leave, because people are *not* really free to walk out. It is so hard for people to be alone; we must always try to find ways of staying together, not of leaving each other.

Your feature films are pessimistic, in that they show that people cannot free themselves or live freely in this society. But your TV *series* Eight Hours are not a Day *is very optimistic: it shows that people can free themselves. Why this striking difference between your films and your* TV *productions?*

Because all the films and plays I've written were intended for an intellectual audience. With them, you can very well be pessimistic and let a film end in hopelessness. An intellectual is completely free to work on the problem with all his intellectual capacities. In the case of the larger public that the TV series reached, it would have been reactionary, even criminal, to give a hopeless picture of the world. Your first obligation is to give your audience strength, to say 'You do still have possibilities – you can make use of your power, because the repressor is dependent on you'. What is an employer without an employee? Nothing. But you can certainly imagine an employee without an employer. For the first time I've made something positive, something with hope, basically on account of this analysis. With an audience of 25 million ordinary people, you cannot allow yourself to do anything else.

The TV series is about a family: a young man, his parents and his grandmother, plus a girl he gets to know and a friend that his grandmother makes. The young man's place of work is important, and the group he works in is almost like another family. I decided to use the same characters throughout the series because people identify with them. When they reappear from episode to episode, viewers are glad to see them again and that helps them participate in the development of the characters – at first in imagination only, but possibly one day in practice too. A series is a better format for describing personal development than a single film. If you describe such a process in a single film, the process ends when the film ends, but the series format makes it easier to carry the issues over into the lives of the viewers. An important element of the TV aesthetic, in fact, is the way that the same programmes come back time and again: the news, the series and so on. This principle should be applied to the features and entertainment programmes you make for TV.

And so your TV work is aesthetically different from your films?

Yes, in the films I've worked according to the aesthetics of pessimism, but in the TV-films I've worked according to the aesthetics of hope, which of course is different. The form also changes when you want to reach a larger group of people. You can use more close-ups in TV than in the cinema, and zooming is often used in TV photography whereas it can be very disturbing on the cinema screen. In film, you prefer to use a tracking-shot. TV-films work more directly with feelings and effects, with real laughter, but films depend more on atmosphere. The TV series was quite popular, but it divided the critics; sometimes opinions differed widely in the same newspaper.

Your theory, then, is that you can allow yourself to be pessimistic in the cinema because you aren't going to reach anyone but the 'art film' public anyway. But isn't that really a rationalisation? Isn't it truer that you have actually become more optimistic? Why couldn't you make optimistic films for the cinema as well as for TV?

You're right, I certainly could do that. The fact that I haven't probably does reflect the fact that I've been more pessimistic than I am now – and the fact that I prefer tragic films when I go to the cinema myself. But my cinema films are made for people like you and me, not for taxi drivers, workers and servants. In a certain sense, it's right to work for a limited audience, so long as you don't do it all the time.

In the TV series, we dealt with problems relating to the workers' mutual solidarity and unity. The employer treats them as isolated individuals, which threatens their solidarity. We have tried to say: unity makes strength. We have documented the proposition in various ways. Basically, we show that the workers do have means of defending themselves, and that they are most effective when they stick together.

We did research for the series for nearly a year; we talked with workers and union people, and visited factories. It was important to us that what we produced would be along the lines of what the workers themselves liked, and so we asked many of them: 'If you saw something about your own situation, what should it be like?' I wrote the series according to the answers we got, and then presented the script to a group of workers we were in touch with. They suggested certain changes. This process took a long time, and the script was rewritten two or three times according to their suggestions.

3: Berlin 1974

Is it true that Fontane's Effi Briest *was your first film project?*

Yes, but in 1969 I couldn't raise the capital, and today I'm thankful for that. At that time I would probably have tried to adapt the story instead of – as now – simply filming the book. Given the little technique and experience I had at that time, my film would probably have looked like the two earlier film versions. There are certain things you shouldn't do as soon as they occur to you: they should be held over until you are *really* ready for them. *Effi Briest* is my dream film, and I decided to make it in black and white because they're the most beautiful colours I know. It's a film that I made exactly as I wished, with no other consideration. If it gets its money back, then that's fine, but that wasn't the reason I made it. It's my most expensive film, and the actual shooting took more than a year.

You see a difference between telling the book's story and filming the book?

Yes, but the difference is mine. I kept close to the novel ... not to the story it tells, but to Fontane's attitude to the story. Of course you could make a lively film just telling the story (a young girl marries an older man, is unfaithful to him, and so on), but if you're just telling a story like that there's no real need to film Fontane's novel. You might as well find a similar story yourself, which is what I did when I made *Martha*, my personal version of the same story. For me, *Effi Briest* is about Fontane's attitude to society, which is re-created in the film by the distance between the audience and what is happening on the screen. There's explicitly something between the two; it may be the author, or even me as director. Through that built-in 'distance', the audience has a chance to discover its own attitude to society.

How do you see Fontane's attitude to society?

That's very easy. He lived in a society whose faults he recognised and could describe very precisely but all the same a society he needed, to which he really wanted to belong. He rejected everybody and found everything alien and yet fought all his life for recognition within this society. And that's also my attitude to society.

That's why you are criticised by so many student-Marxists?

Yes, but not just because of that. Perhaps more because I make something very clear and precise which is very close to their attitudes . . . and this worries them.

Your principle in making films from literature seems related to Jean-Marie Straub's, and your first film was dedicated to Straub, Rohmer and Chabrol. What was your relationship to Straub at the start of your career?

It's difficult because it's a long time ago, and many things have changed since then. But even today I can accept Straub's relationship to his work because he is so extraordinarily serious and yet still has room for improvisation. He is not as inflexible as he appears; the inflexible aspect is his wife Danièle Huillet. Aside from his stubbornness and seriousness, Straub likes to have fun while working. For our Action-Theatre in Munich he directed Ferdinand Bruckner's *Die Krankheit der Jugend*, which is a three-and-a-half-hour play. Straub gradually reduced this to a ten-minute version which was very beautiful and still retained the essence of the original. We worked four months for those ten minutes. Straub used a method where he never said to the actors that they were right or wrong; he simply said 'You know yourselves how it should be'. He directed the actors in such a way that they became aware of themselves, and that I found marvellous. I'm more reserved about his later films. I like best his short films *Machorka-Muff* and *The Bridegroom, the Comedienne and the Pimp*, which stemmed from the Bruckner piece. Also *Not Reconciled* is a very concrete and beautiful work. Straub's weakness is that he continually works against his public. *Othon* is a film which I reject completely.

The Chronicle of Anna Magdalena Bach *achieved a certain amount of public response . . .*

Yes, because of the music. It's a film about Bach music as heard by Straub, and that has a certain objective interest. But *Othon* . . .

In the Bach film there's a principle which I think is also found in Effi Briest: *that of not showing the key scenes, but only referring to them.*

That's right. Had we made 'action scenes', we would have asked the audience to identify with the characters. But having decided beforehand *not* to make such a film, we had to reduce the action scenes to a minimum because they got in the way of the argument. To show the narrative on film is like an author telling a story, but there's a difference. When one reads a book, one creates – as a reader – one's own images, but when a story is told on screen in pictures, then it is concrete and really 'complete'. One is not creative as a member of a film audience, and it was this passivity that I tried to counter in *Effi Briest*. I would prefer people to 'read' the film. It's a film which one cannot simply experience, and which doesn't attack the audience . . . one has to read it. That's the most significant thing about the film.

The clearest example is your handling of the duel scene, where you stress the discussions leading up to the duel but show almost nothing of the duel itself.

That's right, you see hardly anything. The duel is a pretty logical development of the way these people think, but as a duel in itself it is not very important. The only important thing is that it occurs as a consequence of their ideas. The film presents a society where certain things lead to duels, and this particular duel has certain important consequences. I'm interested in what lies before and after the action sequences. The action scenes as such don't interest me.

Actually, the same could be said for the love scenes, although they are hardly described in the novel either. You wonder whether Effi and Major Crampas ever really got into bed together or not.

I guess they did, but the question is open. Fontane doesn't insist on reading it either way: if you want to read it as a case of adultery, then you are free to let your imagination run along those lines, but if your bourgeois morality stops you from doing that, then it's a love story without sexuality. That's how it is in the film too. In my mind, of course they have slept together. But the reader and the viewer must decide in their own imagination whether or not these characters are able to commit this act of adultery.

Why have you concerned yourself so much with women characters? Your attitude surely has nothing to do with Women's Lib?

No, not at all. I'm just as critical of a woman as of a man. The point is that I feel I can express what I want to say better when I use a female character at the centre. Women are more exciting, because on the one hand they are oppressed, and on the other they aren't really, because they use this 'oppression' as terrorisation. Men are so simple: they're more ordinary than women. It's also more amusing to work with women. Men are primitive in their means of expression. Women can show their emotions more, but with men it becomes boring.

Have you seen your early films recently? What do you think of them today?

Not long ago I saw all 23 films in four days, because a book is being published about them. There's a great deal in the first nine films, up to *Beware of a Holy Whore*, which I quite like. The films give a concrete expression of my situation at the time. When you see them all, it's clear that they were made by a person of great sensitivity, aggression and fear. But even so I don't think the first nine films are right. They are too elitist and too private, just made for myself and a few friends ... It's important that I made them, but even if it was right for me to do so, then objectively speaking it wasn't right, because you must respect your audience more than I did. *Beware of a Holy Whore* may also look very private, but it's different. It is a film about film-making, but its real theme is how a group works together.

It's strange to see this film today, when it's clear that it marked the end of the first period of your work, and represents a very real self-criticism. Were you aware when you made it that this was the end and a new beginning?

I wasn't sure that it was a new start, but I knew it had to be the end. With that film we buried the *anti-teater*, which was our first dream. I didn't know what would happen from then on, but I knew it had to change.

I think it would have been better if you rather than Lou Castel had played the film director...

Many people have said that. Maybe it's true, but I wouldn't have been able to make the film the way it is. I would have played him more unsympathetically and that wouldn't have been right, because the film's attitude to that character is already critical and it would have been too much if he'd also been *played* unsympathetically. It may seem better for the initiated if I'd played the director, but for the normal audience Lou Castel was better.

Both your film and Truffaut's Day for Night *deal with the problem that film is something which stands between people and their lives. You even call the art of film a 'holy whore' and warn against it in the title.*

Yes, but there is a mania in film-making. It's not like an ordinary eight-hour-a-day job. Film has to do with everything... Your normal life disappears when you're filming.

Unlike Truffaut, you criticise the view that film is more important than life, and your films after Beware *stem from that criticism...*

Yes, I'm still fighting for true life and reality.

How was it for you when you re-saw The American Soldier?

Gods of the Plague is more personal, but *The American Soldier* is perhaps a more perfect film. It derives from *Love is Colder than Death* and *Gods of the Plague*, and is quite concrete and professionally made. The two earlier films were more exact reconstructions of the atmosphere prevailing among people of that sort at that time in Munich, whereas *The American Soldier* is a more conventional fictional-narrative film, and is full of film quotes from both Hollywood movies and French gangster movies, particularly the films of Raoul Walsh and John Huston. At the time I interpreted the film more politically, but now I think the 'film quotes' were more important.

Your earlier films evoke for me the relationship between the police and the Baader-Meinhof group...

That's all to do with the atmosphere in Germany when I made those films. But at that time I couldn't make a film specifically about the Baader-Meinhof group, and even today I would find it difficult. What Claude Chabrol has done in *Nada* is really quite false; it isn't the film about anarchists I'd hoped for. I think highly of Chabrol and I was therefore very disappointed that he was as cynical in his attitude to the terrorists as to society ... that's a little too easy.

Why don't you make a film with that theme?

It's difficult because I can't quite define my attitude. If I clarify my position, then I'm sure that I'll make a film about anarchists sometime.

On the one hand you can understand public attitudes to the anarchists' use of violence, the way they work against their own goal; on the other hand, you can sympathise with the anarchists' situation, and their criticism of aspects of our society ...

True enough, but I'm very interested in finding out how one can use the strength those people have. Now it's very important to me to make very positive films, and they are very clever people. They have great intellectual potential, but also an over-sensitive despair which I don't know how one would use constructively. Because they don't know how themselves either, they have started using those stupid methods, and so even with their strength they haven't really progressed. They've been terribly impatient. They thought the revolution must happen tomorrow and because it hasn't they've flipped. You have to reckon in centuries, but they thought only in decades. But I don't really know what their alternative is, and that's why I couldn't make a film about them. *Nada* isn't a real film because Chabrol hasn't given it the degree of despair which is necessary. It doesn't interest me, because he looks at both parties from the outside.

4: Frankfurt/Cannes 1975

Films like Effi Briest *and* Martha *are controversial because they depict women who accept – even desire – their own repression.*

Most women have been brought up to be completely satisfied when these mechanisms of regression take hold. That doesn't mean that they don't suffer under them ... of course they do. How one reacts has a lot to do with her personality. I know some fairly emancipated women who enjoy being repressed and at the same time fight against their repression. It's a state full of contradictions.

Militant Women's Liberationists have been particularly critical of Petra von Kant *and* Effi Briest.

Some women do criticise me very sharply, and call me a misogynist – an accusation that I always repudiate. I am not a woman-hater, and such accusations can only come from people who (consciously or not) choose to overlook what my films actually say. Even in *Martha*, where Martha herself to a great extent shares the blame for what happens to her and in some ways enjoys it, even there it seems to me entirely clear that the basis for her reaction lies in her upbringing. From that point of view, *Martha* and all my other films are *for* women, not against them. But almost all of them hate *Petra von Kant* – at least, those who have the kind of problem that the film is about but won't admit it. I can't help it.

In find my own attitude to women quite honest. All in all, I find that women behave just as despicably as men do, and I try to illustrate the reasons for this: namely, that we have been led astray by our upbringing and by the society we live in. My depiction of these conditions is not misogynistic. It is honest. At the same time, though, I don't think it's for me to say how women should set about liberating themselves. Every woman must decide that for herself. All I can do is point out that certain things are wrong, and that something must be done about them.

In connection with your portrayal of women, you have sometimes used cannibalism or vampirism as a metaphor – for example, in Martha *and in your play* The Burning Village.

That's a Catholic motif, and it has something to do with my friends Kurt Raab and Peer Raben, both of whom had Catholic upbringings. The entire Catholic religion is built on such bizarre questions as the signification of bread and wine. I am strangely drawn to cannibalism. It's not a positive attraction; maybe it's a negative one. Whatever, there is an attraction of some sort which I'm trying to work my way through, even though I wasn't raised as a Catholic myself.

I was brought up in accordance with the theories of Rudolf Steiner, which are not religious but based on the pedagogical principle that children shouldn't be forced to do anything, but should always decide for themselves what they think is right. They are allowed to do whatever interests them, and are not forced to do things that don't interest them. The idea is that children should grow up like little flowers.

And that suited you?

Even that was too much compulsion for me. I grew up in a family where there was none of that at all, where no one worried about when I ate and slept and that sort of thing. The only times I experienced coercion were when I visited neighbours or relations, never when I was with my own father and mother. From the time I was four, all my decisions were left entirely to me. And so when I first went to school, I wasn't used to being punctual or obeying rules. I always hated that.

Do you plan to go on with this staggering rate of production, or are you considering taking things a little easier?

Sometimes I think of taking it easier, but at the same time I've discovered that work is necessary for me. I get very depressed when I'm not working. For the time being, my plan is to make my thirtieth film when I turn thirty. I've achieved a lot of the things that directors aspire to, I've had more success than most and I earn more than most – but none of that in itself has made me any happier. I can't see any reason to be happy when I see how people live. When I meet people in the streets and in railway stations, see their faces and their lives, it fills me with despair. I often want to scream out loud.

People often criticise my films for being pessimistic. There are certainly plenty of reasons for being pessimistic, but I don't see my films that way. They are founded in the belief that revolution doesn't belong on the cinema screen, but outside, in the world. When I show people, on the screen, the ways that things can go wrong, my aim is to warn them that that's the way things *will* go if they don't change their lives. Never mind if a film ends pessimistically; if it exposes certain mechanisms clearly enough to show people how exactly they work, then the ultimate effect is not pessimistic. I never try to reproduce reality in a film. My goal is to reveal such mechanisms in a way that makes people realise the necessity of changing their own reality.

5: Berlin 1977

What I've long wanted to discuss with you is your attitude to masochism, especially in relation to the films Satan's Brew *and* Shadow of Angels.

There's no such thing as masochism without sadism. And relationships between people are always sado-masochistic as a direct result of their upbringing. That rule also applies to the individual who is not just a masochist or a sadist: it isn't that easy.

If one looks at the reasons for Walter Kranz's masochism in Satan's Brew *one doesn't really learn anything about his upbringing.*

Of course one knows something. We see his meeting with his parents, and from the way he treats them we can see how they have treated him and why he must live under such pressure that he really rejects his parents.

How have they treated him?

As well as they could. They've tried to suppress him, so that later he has – as far as he could – tried to develop. And it's exactly because of this that he stays small, because of the way they've treated him. The film provides an opportunity for the relationship to be thought through to the end. Of course, one doesn't need to do that. The more films I see here at this Berlin Festival, the more I'm really sure that the way I describe people in my films is more accurate and true. These films today don't portray people. They show people as religious beings, and even then they're missing a dramatic story within the framework of the film. I really don't understand today's films.

Do you really mean, then, that the reason for Walter Kranz's masochism is that his self-assertion is false and he wants to be punished in order to be suppressed again, as he was by his parents?

It really is like that. Everyone who comes into the world is not taken seriously as a human being, because obviously it's difficult for an adult to take such a little unformed thing seriously. As time passes, the parent becomes the figure which the child in one respect accepts as dominant, which means that all through their lives they will accept dominant figures while at the same time trying to destroy this dominance in order to exist. Actually a child develops a dual need for dominance and destruction, which is to say that one becomes sadistic and masochistic at the same time.

If one looks at some of your other films or characters, for example Marlene in The Bitter Tears of Petra von Kant, *or your own character in* Shadow of Angels, *perhaps there's another reason for people's masochism. They are so destroyed that they are simply unable to change their lives or the world around them.*

It's very complicated because I mean that only those individuals who can accept their own masochism are on the way to being healthy. It's when people suppress their problems that they're really sick. They ought to live their lives outwardly. When you live with problems rather than hiding them, then you can analyse them and overcome them. And in that way masochism can lead to something positive. Self-knowledge is essential. Take the Jews, for instance. For hundreds of years they've shown their masochism, but at the same time it's brought them so much further than other people. It's no coincidence that the two most important figures of our time – Marx and Freud – were both Jews. The Jews as a race have lived through a very masochistic experience and from it they have produced many people who have contributed to human knowledge. This will sound terribly anti-semitic, because one is always misunderstood; but if you're always trying to avoid being misunderstood, you're finished.

But this Jewish masochism is probably also because you can't change your conditioning, so you're bound not just to accept it but to enjoy it so as to get something more out of life.

Yes, to enjoy the pain is always cleverer than simply to suffer it. That goes for all minorities, by the way, but so far as I can see only the Jews have exploited it. Other minorities haven't suffered in quite the same way, but they've suffered more inwardly and so they haven't gained as much from their suffering as the Jews.

By other minorities you also mean your own minority, homosexuals?

Yes, of course. But homosexuals have been very self-pitying, and also most of them are dominated by a sense of shame, which the Jews haven't had. The Jews have never been ashamed of being Jews, whereas homosexuals have been stupid enough to be ashamed of their homosexuality. The Jews have believed that they are God's chosen people, which comes from their experience.

But many people share that attitude. You find both men and women homosexuals who think they're here to save the world.

Various groups have split up now. Also among gays you find those who don't use their homosexuality to indulge in self-pity, but take the 'black is beautiful' line. But that only goes hand in hand with the awareness that one is suffering, and this awareness means that one can't enjoy the suffering, which is the most difficult thing. It isn't easy to accept that suffering can also be beautiful.

Under what circumstances can suffering be beautiful?

Physically? Well, it's difficult. It's something you can only understand if you dig deeply into yourself. If you mean you don't know from your own experience then I can't explain it.

How are you going to tackle the 'German Jewish complex' as it's dealt with in Gustav Freitag's novel Soll und Haben?

I've not got permission to film it. The Controller of Plays for Westdeutsche Rundfunk has said no to the series. And I'm sure it's the first time in German television history that a controller has made such a decision without seeing the material. We've been working on the project for eighteen months and there is a 30-page treatment where we've explained how we'll tackle the subject. On top of that we've written three scripts for the series – but he's simply refused to read the material and won't enter into any kind of discussion. He just said no, and that makes me mad as hell because the novel explains German history from the middle of the last century to the breakthrough of National Socialism. Also it expresses the complete opposite of what Mr Joachim Fest did in his Hitler film [*Hitler – a Career*], which is terribly reactionary and really tries to let the bourgeoisie off the hook. Because Nazism is quite clearly an extension of the bourgeoisie's position, and if Fest doesn't show that in his film it's because it still exists today.

My project was a ten-part TV series in which we were trying to trace the characters through the whole history of the period up to the present. We wanted to show that National Socialism wasn't an accident but a logical extension of the German bourgeoisie's attitudes, which haven't altered to this day. And it's obvious that if one takes that line one's work will be jeopardised. This is what I've come to realise, and to accuse me of anti-semitism is nothing more than a clever pretext, since my aim is simply to show what anti-semitism has brought about. It's possible that some asides in Freitag's novel *are* anti-semitic, but it's precisely because of them that the book can be used to portray anti-semitism – and surely the journalist Freitag is not anti-semitic when he describes ghetto life and the hopeless situation the Jews are in, where they have to be negative in order to exist? I don't find it anti-semitic to describe the depths a Jew may have to sink to in order to exist. Actually I find it anti-semitic to say about Jews – and other minorities – that just because they are minorities they are blameless. To believe that is dangerous and fascist. The best way to describe the majority's view of a minority is to show the kinds of failure and cruel pressures an individual member of that minority may be forced to accept.

But isn't that exactly the objection made about some of your 'women's films'?

It's precisely the same. If one is looking seriously at women, one has to take into account their faults – what they've had to do to compete with men. It may not be easy to sympathise with them for this – but you don't hate women because of it. I find the people who don't like women are the ones who always show them as beautiful, elegant – and that's because they don't take women seriously. But German films are suffering increasingly from the committee structure – because the financiers are afraid of films they don't understand. And when there's suddenly a very personal and original film – like Walter Bockmayer's first film, *Jane bleibt Jane* – there's a danger of it being totally neglected. Ten years ago that film would have created a sensation because then we had a cultural climate which would have recognised its special qualities. Now the film is rejected; in Berlin it's neither the official German festival entry nor in the market. What people want now is middle-of-the-road, impersonal 'perfection', the kind of thing which doesn't upset anybody. *Jane bleibt Jane* is a very painful but funny film, with a couple of scenes which will certainly go into film history. It's about an old woman who is terrified of old age and starts to imagine that she's married to Tarzan and lives that fantasy to the bitter end. And in describing what fear of old age does to an old woman like that the film really questions the sickness in our society which creates that kind of fear in people.

The last film I saw of yours was Chinese Roulette, *which had the most perfectly realised camerawork.*

It's the first of my films where I don't just tell the story with the help of actors. People's relationships are built up out of ritual and repeated patterns. We didn't just want to show how people behave or what they do with their faces; we wanted to show it with camera movement. Because when the camera moves a great deal round something that's dead, it's shown to be dead. Then you can create a longing for something that's alive. I tried to make a film that takes artificiality to its limits, precisely to examine that question. I'm sure there's no other film in the history of cinema with as many camera movements, tracking shots and movements around the actors as we had in this one. I made the film first because it looks like a film about marriage as an institution, and then because this is such an infantile notion that you can show more about how false marriage is.

Do the numerous mirror shots in the film express the longing for things to be reborn?

I hope so. That's how I see it: the rituals go on in the mirrors, where they are broken up, and one hopes that these fractures are so pronounced that the audience unconsciously prepares itself to break with rituals of this kind. Of course, it's too much to ask that a film should have this kind of impact. Take for example Robert Bresson's *Le Diable, Probablement*, which is the most shattering film I've seen in this Berlin Festival. I think it's a major film; but then people say – but what if you show a film like this to the man in the street and he doesn't understand it? First of all, I think that's wrong. But even if it's true, doesn't it mean that in the future – and this world will probably last for another few thousand years – this film will be more important than all the rubbish which is now considered important but which never really goes deep enough? The questions Bresson asks will never be unimportant.

What about the problems raised in Bresson's film – are they rejecting all existing political forms?

Yes, rejecting every commitment. Because commitment for the film's young characters – whom he seems to understand so well – is mainly an escape into an 'occupation' which keeps that commitment alive. An escape from the awareness that everything goes on regardless of you and your commitment.

You seem to have changed your position. When you made the television films Eight Hours are not a Day, *you still believed in the importance of commitment.*

I still do – don't get me wrong. I'm always saying that as long as I live I will do whatever I can. But at the same time I could also say it's meaningless, and in the last analysis I'd probably be right. All the values one has, and the fear and pain linked to them, are ultimately quite unimportant when set against higher values. You have to understand that everything is unimportant before you can become *really* committed, because then it becomes a fearless commitment.

I was a little surprised by the ending of Chinese Roulette, *with the procession and that Catholic hymn they were singing.*

It's not Catholic, it only sounds like it. Peer Raben wrote it – he also sings it – and it comes from the end of *Gods of the Plague* if I remember rightly. It appears in *Niklashauser Fahrt* in a different version. The problem is, when you're working with the interior of a character you reach a point where you really understand their need for religion. Since I'm not a second Marx or Freud who can offer people alternatives, I have to let them keep their own wrong feelings. And I don't believe that melodramatic feelings are laughable – they should be taken absolutely seriously.

But in Chinese Roulette *it's you who put the hymn at the end of the film, which makes it seem like an expression of your need for religion ...*

Did you see the film with or without the concluding text? Along with the procession and the music there should be a text – the text of the marriage vows. It looks as though a few prints have been made without this text. This happened at the Paris Festival when a few critics, who liked the film, were confused by this apparently religious ending. But when the text is there, the religious music and the procession have the effect of an escape ritual – a false ritual. And then the music is not a ploy by me as director but a way of describing people's hopeless attempts to escape. The procession which ends the film just happened – I didn't stage it. We were about to shoot a scene of the house with the lights showing through the windows, at dusk, when this procession passed by. Michael Ballhaus turned the camera on them as they passed the house. At first I thought that was nice of him but it didn't interest me. Then during the night I began to think how strange it was that in front of that house, where everything is possible, a procession should suddenly just pass by, making the precise symbol of what these people needed. That was a good enough reason to include it in the film. But a procession by itself would probably have looked too puritanical, so I asked Peer Raben to put some music to it. When you've looked at people for over an hour and a half in their stiffest and most formal rituals, it's obvious what their religion is. Also it's just a pure formality.

Since we're talking about endings, there are two endings to Mother Küsters' Trip to Heaven: *the original ending, where Mother Küsters is gunned down, which is also explained by a concluding text; and a later version with a happy ending, where the terrorist lets her live and she goes home with the night porter. I think this second version was shown in Britain and the United States.*

Yes. And really I prefer the so-called happy ending. I made it because many people told me that the first ending was too hard. So I tried a gentler ending, which I prefer because it is actually tougher than the original. The first ending, with the text, is perhaps more intellectual – but the other one affects people more emotionally.

Doesn't the first ending conclude the story in a more uncompromising way?

Not at all. When the woman has fought for something for so long – and even gets some sympathy for it – but has to give up because no one will support her, what happens with the first ending is almost the worst thing that could happen, and there's no consolation at the end of the story. I think it's a really clinical ending which turns against the system that the film itself is criticising.

As I understand Nabokov's novel Despair, *its main theme is the 'identity problem' as an art form – something you've touched on before, in* Satan's Brew, *for example. Is that why you filmed it?*

The reason I made *Despair* came from an awareness that in everyone's life there comes a point where not only the mind but the body too understands that it's 'all over'. I want to go on with my life, but there will be no new feelings or experiences for me. Everything will be repeats, and the fun I have will be the fun I have forced myself to 'enjoy', what I know should be fun. One no longer gets a naive pleasure out of things. At this point most people start to rearrange their lives. They go in for politics and start to defend the system. *Despair*, for me, is about someone who doesn't stop at that point, but tells himself that a life which consists only of repeats is no life at all. And instead of committing suicide, as the guy does in Bresson's new film, he openly decides to become insane. He kills a man he thinks is his double and tries to take over his identity, even though he knows very well that they are not look-alikes. He moves of his own free will into the land of the insane, because he reckons that that's where he can start a new life. Whether it's possible or not I don't know, because I haven't yet been quite that mad. But I can well imagine that you have to take that step. In a way it's also about a suicide. He's got to kill himself first, and that's why he kills the other person, who he imagines to be his double.

This is the first film you've made with another scriptwriter — Tom Stoppard from England. How did it work out?

Well, it was meant to be an English film, so it was very important to work with an English scriptwriter. I met Stoppard five times when we were writing the script. We had long 'battles'. The funny thing was that Stoppard suddenly reached the point when he wanted the two roles — the main part and the double — to be played by the same person. Which for me was impossible. The thing didn't interest me at all if it was simply about a person who met another man who looked like him. In fact, it's quite a complicated story when you think about it, but as a film it's very simple.

There's a different perspective in the book...

Yes, when you read the book you're not quite sure that the characters are not look-alikes. But when you see the film, it's clear from the start that Dirk Bogarde and Klaus Löwitsch don't resemble one another. When you read the book it seems even more abstract than the film, and I really do think it's possible to make a proper film of Nabokov's story.

Did you have any other differences of opinion with Stoppard?

No. I wrote a few things into the script which he approved but didn't like. Dirk Bogarde told him that his work was greatly respected by everybody but once shooting began he would have to stay in the background and believe in our work without our having to follow the script 100 per cent. While directing I tried to forget the script and return to the novel, which has that darkness and strangeness which wasn't in the script. It is the scriptwriter's job to provide material for the director; and the better the material the better chance there is of the director creating his own fantasies. Under certain circumstances one could say that the more the film gets away from the material, the better. The less breadth the script gives your fantasy and the easier it is to read as a script, the worse it really is as a screenplay.

With your huge output, has the point arrived where you've run out of ideas? Your last three films – Bolwieser, Frauen in New York *and* Despair – *have been based on literary works.*

Well, I've filmed other people's work before – *Effi Briest, Pioneers in Ingolstadt, Fear of Fear*. When I film other writers' work, it's because I could have written them. That's to say, they're concerned with the same problems I concern myself with. My own ideas I get all the time – that's the least of my worries. I have to hold back my own ideas because every day I find three stories which could make a film – *stories* I've never been short of. What can sometimes be a problem is the experience of the mechanics of film-making. When it becomes mechanical, the medium loses its original fascination. But with *Despair* I really had a problem, because Dirk Bogarde is such a marvellous actor to work with that every day was a challenge. In future, I'd like to work with actors who – without being false – can express what I want and at the same time bring so much of themselves to the role that the work never ceases to fascinate me.

Does that mean you have more or less abandoned working with your regular group?

To a certain extent. I've certainly finished working with actors who don't contribute anything themselves. I have to make my next film abroad because I can't do what I want in my own country – and that means I have to work with other actors.

What about your plans to film Freud's Der Mann Moses?

I'm going to try to make a television series from it. The television medium is fantastically right for a work with a psychoanalytical basis. What with the news, sport and TV drama with 'nice' ladies in hats and lots of make-up, it's all plastic. I think TV as a medium is only properly used when you show things which go straight to the viewers – talk directly to the family sitting in front of the screen. It sounds idiotic to say that I want to popularise Freud, but I would like to make him more accessible – for those people who can't afford psychoanalysis. I believe, by the way, that it's easier for people to have that experience in the cinema, because there you're surrounded by strangers whereas with TV you're usually watching with your family.

In the cinema you're much more defenceless because of the darkness and isolation, whereas with television you've always got an excuse for not concentrating.

It depends how you show what people don't want to watch. You can show it in a way which makes them reject it. But another way is to learn how to show viewers the things they don't want to see in such a way that they *will* watch because it's excitingly made. Whether I'm allowed to make this TV series or not is still uncertain. WDR have recently developed a new organisational structure where the power is more centralised. They've done away with small groups who could fight for a particular project. The whole arts department is suffering under this structure – everything is 'kaput', everything is divided ... you know, Germany is really a very tiny, provincial country. I'm afraid about developments over the next few years, because Nazism is creeping back in new forms – just like a repeat of the 1930s.

How conscious are you that your films find inspiration in pre-1933 German culture? Mother Küsters' Trip to Heaven *is derived from* Mutter Krausens Fahrt ins Glück, *Franz Biberkopf in* Fox *comes from the main character in the novel* Berlin Alexanderplatz, *and* Bolwieser *is from Oscar Maria Graf, who fled the Nazis in 1933.*

True, but it's not just for me that this is an important period – there's a whole stream of new directors, Herzog, Wenders, Kluge and two or three others. If we'd oriented ourselves to what was being made elsewhere in the world, we'd have been making rubbish. We had to start where things ended in our own country in order to pick up the pieces. With me it's probably more noticeable. I'm not as self-absorbed as Herzog, but even he gets inspiration from the old myths, and Wenders has also tried to use stories from films made before 1933. The directors who came just before us were very much involved in the 'New Wave'. And look at the young Czech directors who went elsewhere for their inspiration and never made it. Before I started to make films I was interested in the pre-1933 period in my theatre work, and I worked with expressionists – but like the people from that period I feel that I have to go into exile if I'm going to go on existing ...

Interviews 3 and 5 translated from the Danish by Søren Fischer. English translations of interviews 1, 2 and 4 revised by Tony Rayns.

Documentation

Tony Rayns

Abbreviations
Fassbinder's name is abbreviated throughout to 'RWF'. Technical credits are abbreviated as follows: *d*–Director, *sc*–Screenplay, *ph*–Photography, *col*–Colour, *b&w*–Black-and-White, *ed*–Editor, *des*–Designer, *m*–Music, *l.p*–Leading Players, *p.c*–Production Company.

Biography

Rainer Werner Fassbinder born 31 May 1946 in the Bavarian spa Bad Wörishofen. Father (Hellmuth Fassbinder) a doctor, mother (Liselotte) a translator, and subsequently an actress in many of RWF's films under the name Lilo Pempeit. Educated at the Rudolf Steiner School and at secondary schools in Augsburg and Munich. When his parents divorced he stayed with his mother, who often sent him to the cinema while she worked. Left school in 1964, worked in various jobs and then attended a private drama school where he met Hanna Schygulla. With her, joined the *Action-Theater* group (a 'fringe' theatre in Munich's Müllerstrasse) in mid-1967. Jean-Marie Straub's film *The Bridegroom, the Comedienne and the Pimp* includes the entirety of his production of Ferdinand Bruckner's *Krankheit der Jugend* with the company (including RWF) in this theatre. RWF's first original play produced in April 1968; *Action-Theater* closed by police in May 1968. RWF and nine others from the original group (including Hanna Schygulla, Peer Raben and Kurt Raab) go on to found *anti-teater*, eventually finding a base in the back room of a Schwabing bar. *Anti-teater* lost its home at the end of 1969 and began working without a permanent base, but by that time RWF had already begun making feature films. In subsequent years, RWF has worked in the theatre in Munich, Bremen, Nuremberg, Bochum, Berlin and Frankfurt, produced a number of radio plays and acted in his own and others' films, as well as directing and writing films for TV and the cinema. In 1970 he married the *anti-teater* actress Ingrid Caven; they are now divorced. In 1971 he founded the independent film production company Tango Film, for which nearly all his independent cinema features have been made; in 1975 he founded an additional company, Albatros Produktion, primarily for co-productions. In the spring of 1974, RWF (with co-directors Kurt Raab and Roland Petri) took over the Frankfurt TAT (Theater am Turm) and installed a 'stock company' of stars from his films and colleagues from the *anti-teater* for a projected three-year residency. The experiment ended acrimoniously barely a year later, since when RWF has returned to live in Munich and devoted his energies more single-mindedly to films than to theatre. His controversial play 'about Frankfurt', *Der Müll, die Stadt und der Tod, oder Frankenstein am Main* (*The Garbage, the City and Death, or Frankenstein am Main*), unproduced at the TAT, was filmed in 1976 by Daniel Schmid as *Shadow of Angels*. Since 1976, RWF's films have relied less on actors from his stock company for their casts, and have occasionally had scripts by other writers.

His first big-budget film, *Despair*, was made in English. At the end of 1978, RWF began directing the photography on his own films.

Filmography

Note: RWF has produced most of his cinema films himself, without credit. He also edited many of his early films, under the pseudonym Franz Walsch. (The latter name, also used as a character name in some of the films, derives from two of RWF's favourite 'sources': 'Franz' from Franz Biberkopf, the central character in Alfred Döblin's novel *Berlin Alexanderplatz* – and the name of the character played by RWF in *Fox*; 'Walsch' from the name of the American film director Raoul Walsh.)

Cinema and TV films as director

1965: *Der Stadtstreicher*
d/sc–RWF. ph–Josef Jung. b&w. l.p–Christoph Roser, Susanne Schimkus, Michael Fengler, Thomas Fengler, Irm Hermann, RWF. p.c.–Roser-Film. 16 mm. 10 mins.
A man finds a gun in a Munich alleyway, and tries to get rid of it again.
'Arose from my love of Rohmer's *Le Signe du Lion*' – RWF.

1966: *Das kleine Chaos*
d/sc–RWF. ph–Michael Fengler. b&w. l.p–Marite Greiselis, Christoph Roser, Lilo Pempeit, Greta Rehfeld, RWF. p.c.–Roser-Film. 35 mm. 9 mins. (originally 12).
Three young people selling magazine subscriptions enter a woman's home and rob her.
'... a little like Godard' – RWF.

1969: *Liebe ist kälter als der Tod (Love is Colder than Death)*
'For Claude Chabrol, Eric Rohmer, Jean-Marie Straub, Lino and Cuncho. The track along the Landsberger Strasse was provided by Jean-Marie Straub.'
d/sc–RWF. ph–Dietrich Lohmann. b&w. ed–Franz Walsch. des–Ulli Lommel, RWF. m–Peer Raben, Holger Münzer. l.p–Ulli Lommel (*Bruno*), Hanna Schygulla (*Joanna*), RWF (*Franz*), Hans Hirschmüller (*Peter*), Katrin Schaake (*Woman on train*), Peter Berling (*Illegal Arms Dealer*), Hannes Gromball (*Joanna's Customer*), Gisela Otto, Ingrid Caven and Ursula Strätz (*Prostitutes*), Irm Hermann (*Sunglasses Seller*), Les Olvides (*Georges*), Wil Rabenbauer (*Jürgen*), Peter Moland (*Leader of Syndicate Hearing*), Anastassios Karalas (*The Turk*), Rudolf Waldemar Brem (*Motorcycle Cop*), Yaak Karsunke (*Inspector*), Monika Stadler (*Girl*), Kurt Raab (*Look-out*). p.c.–anti-teater-X-Film. 35 mm. 88 mins.
'At the start a syndicate wants Franz (acted by me) to work for it. But he only wants to work for himself and keep all of what he earns. Bruno (acted by Lommel) works for the syndicate and is sent after Franz. He can react quite differently from Franz, because he knows that he isn't alone. Franz happens to like Bruno. But at the same time he doesn't realise it. He invites him to his place and wants him to sleep with his girl, just because he likes him and doesn't question his liking. But then he can't question anything... just like Bruno, who does what he's told. And Joanna the girl does the same. She (acted by

Hanna Schygulla) is actually the main thing. Her character reveals that she is stuck in middle-classness, despite her profession, even worse than the others: she wants to save her bourgeois relationship with Franz by being his whore and even by betraying Bruno and a bank-robbery to the police. She would rather be alone than share Franz with Bruno. She just can't stand that' – RWF.

1969: *Katzelmacher*
'For Marie Luise Fleisser. Motto: It's better to make new mistakes than to organise old ones to the point of general unconsciousness (Yaak Karsunke).'
d/sc–RWF. *ph*–Dietrich Lohmann. *b&w*. *ed*–Franz Walsch. *des*–RWF. *m*–Peer Raben (after Franz Schubert). *l.p*–Hanna Schygulla (*Marie*), Lilith Ungerer (*Helga*), Elga Sorbas (*Rosy*), Doris Mattes (*Gunda*), RWF (*Jorgos*), Rudolf Waldemar Brem (*Paul*), Hans Hirschmüller (*Erich*), Harry Baer (*Franz*), Peter Moland (*Peter*), Hannes Gromball (*Klaus*), Irm Hermann (*Elisabeth*), Katrin Schaake (*Woman on Landstrasse*). *p.c*–anti-teater-X-film. 35 mm. 88 mins.
'Katzelmacher' is Bavarian slang for a foreigner, especially someone from the South, who is supposed to enjoy great sexual potency. Greek immigrant worker Jorgos, illiterate and inarticulate in German, arrives in Munich and finds himself the centre of attention among a gang of backyard layabouts and their girls; the girls are attracted to him, but the men despise and resent him, and finally beat him up.
'I've been conscious of the *Gastarbeiter* (immigrant worker) problem for a long time .. I have a definite affinity with them' – RWF.

1969: *Götter der Pest (Gods of the Plague)*
d/sc–RWF. *ph*–Dietrich Lohmann. *b&w*. *ed*–Franz Walsch. *des*–Kurt Raab. *m*–Peer Raben. *l.p*–Harry Baer (*Franz*), Hanna Schygulla (*Joanna*), Margarethe von Trotta (*Margarethe*), Günther Kaufmann (*Günther*), Carla Aulaulu (*Carla*), Ingrid Caven (*Magdalena Fuller*), Jan George (*Cop*), Marian Seidowski (*Marian*), Yaak Karsunke (*Inspector*), Micha Cochina (*Joe*), Hannes Gromball (*Supermarket Manager*), Lilith Ungerer (*Girl in First Café*), Katrin Schaake (*Owner of Second Café*), Lilo Pempeit (*Mother*), RWF (*Porno Buyer*), Irm Hermann, Peter Moland, Doris Mattes. *p.c*–anti-teater. 35 mm. 91 mins.
Released from jail, Franz feels his way back into the Munich underworld: rejecting the possessive Joanna, more comfortable with Margarethe but happiest with Günther (known as 'Gorilla'), who shot Franz' police-informer brother. After Franz and Günther have raided a supermarket, Joanna betrays them to the police.
'*Gods of the Plague* is a fairly precise film in dealing with the feeling of a particular time ... it was really like that in that strange post-revolutionary period in 1970' –RWF.

1969: *Warum läuft Herr R amok? (Why Does Herr R Run Amok?)*
d–Michael Fengler, RWF. *sc*–improvised by Michael Fengler, RWF. *ph*–Dietrich Lohmann. *col*. *ed*–Franz Walsch, Michael Fengler. *des*–Kurt Raab. *m*–'Geh' nicht vorbei', by Christian Anders. *l.p*–Kurt Raab (*Herr R*), Lilith Ungerer (*His wife*), Amadeus Fengler (*Their Son*), Franz Maron (*Boss*), Harry Baer, Peter Moland and Lilo Pempeit (*Colleagues at Office*), Hanna Schygulla (*Schoolfriend*), Mr and Mrs Sterr (*Father and Mother*), Peer Raben (*Schoolfriend*), Carla Aulaulu and Eva Pampuch (*Salesgirls in Record Shop*), Ingrid Caven, Doris Mattes, Irm Hermann and Hannes Gromball (*Neighbours*), Peter Hamm and Jochen Pinkert (*Inspectors*), Eva Madelung (*Boss's Sister*). *p.c*–anti-teater, for Maran-Film (SDR). 35 mm (blown up from 16 mm). 88 mins.

Technical designer R is happily married, with a child, and enjoys every middle-class comfort. One evening he calmly kills his wife, son and a neighbour, and next day commits suicide at the office.
The only *anti-teater* film in which stylisation is sacrificed in favour of a more orthodox 'realism': the cast improvised their dialogue under Fengler and Fassbinder's joint direction. Its theme is partially resumed in *Fear of Fear*, in which Kurt Raab plays a neighbour who commits suicide.

1970: *Rio das Mortes*
d–RWF. *sc*–RWF, from an idea by Volker Schlöndorff. *ph*–Dietrich Lohmann. *col*. *ed*–Thea Eymèsz. *des*–Kurt Raab. *m*–Peer Raben. *l.p*–Hanna Schygulla (*Hanna*), Michael König (*Michel*), Günther Kaufmann (*Günther*), Katrin Schaake (*Katrin, Hanna's friend*), Joachim von Mengershausen (*Joachim, Katrin's friend*), Lilo Pempeit (*Günther's Mother*), Franz Maron (*Hanna's Uncle*), Harry Baer (*Michel's Colleague*), Marius Aicher (*Master*), Carla Aulaulu (*Customer*), Walter Sedlmayr (*Secretary*), Ulli Lommel (*Car Dealer*), Monika Stadler (*Travel Agency Assistant*), Hanna Axmann-Rezzori (*Patroness*), Ingrid Caven, Kerstin Dobbertin, Magdalena Montezuma and Elga Sorgas (*Hanna's Colleagues*), Kurt Raab (*Petrol Pump Attendant*), Rudolf Waldemar Brem (*Bar Patron*), Carl Amery (*Librarian*), RWF (*Discotheque-goer*), Eva Pampuch (*His friend*). *p.c*–Janus Film und Fernsehen/anti-teater-X-film. 16 mm. 84 mins. (at 25 f.p.s.)
Reunited with his former schoolfriend Michel after serving in the navy, Günther revives a childhood dream of going to Peru in search of lost treasure. Michel's girlfriend Hanna opposes the plan, which makes little progress until Michel and Günther find a patroness willing to finance the trip. At the airport Hanna draws a gun on the two men, but pockets it again, leaving them free to go.
'If it were a film like the others I've made, she would have shot them . . . then she would have taken it all as seriously as, in fact, she does' – RWF.

1970: *Whity*
'For Peter Berling'
d/sc–RWF. *ph*–Michael Ballhaus. *col*. Cinemascope. *ed*–Franz Walsch, Thea Eymèsz. *des*–Kurt Raab. *m*–Peer Raben. *l.p*–Günther Kaufmann (*Whity*), Hanna Schygulla (*Hanna*), Ulli Lommel (*Frank*), Harry Baer (*Davy*), Katrin Schaake (*Katherine*), Ron Randell (*Mr. Nicholson*), Thomas Blanco (*Fake Mexican Doctor*), Stefano Capriati (*Judge*), Elaine Baker (*Whity's Mother*), Mark Salvage (*Sheriff*), Helga Ballhaus (*Judge's Wife*), Kurt Raab (*Pianist*), RWF (*Guest in Saloon*). *p.c*–Atlantis Film/anti-teater-X-film. 35 mm. 95 mins.
The mulatto Whity works for the Nicholson family: Ben, his half-wit sons by his first marriage and his second wife Kate. Prostitute-cum-saloon-singer Hanna makes Whity conscious of his situation for the first time, and urges him to murder the Nicholsons. But Whity is unable to act; he and Hanna dance into the desert together.
'*Whity* is a stylised primitive melodrama, a mixture of Southern and Western epics, archetypal decadence clichés and pompousness, a filmic ritual of downfall; the whites' history in a white mask . . . the expression of an entirely detached pessimism, of a now completely secondary experience' – Alf Brustellin, *Süddeutsche Zeitung*.

1970: *Die Niklashauser Fahrt*
d/sc–RWF, Michael Fengler. *ph*–Dietrich Lohmann. *col*. *ed*–Thea Eymèsz, Franz Walsch. *des*–Kurt Raab. *m*–Peer Raben, Amon Düül II. *l.p*–Michael König (*Hans*

Böhm), Michael Gordon (*Antonio*), RWF (*Black Monk*), Hanna Schygulla (*Johanna*), Walter Sedlmayr (*Priest*), Margit Carstensen (*Margarethe*), Franz Maron (*Her Husband*), Kurt Raab (*Bishop*), Günther Rupp (*His Counsellor*), Karl Scheydt (*Citizen*), Günther Kaufmann (*Farmers' Leader*), Siggi Graue and Michael Fengler (*Farmers*), Ingrid Caven (*Screaming Girl*), Elga Sorbas (*Helpless Girl*), Carla Aulaulu (*Epileptic Girl*), Peer Raben (*Monsignor*), Peter Berling (*Executioner*), Magdalena Montezuma (*Penthesilea*). p.c–Janus Film und Fernsehen (for WDR). 16 mm. 86 mins. (at 25 f.p.s.).

Suggested by an actual historical occurrence: in 1476 Hans Böhm proclaimed that he had been visited by the Virgin Mary and embarked on a programme of radical social reforms until the armies of the church arrested and executed him four months later. Fassbinder's version is 'timeless' in the same way as Godard's *Weekend*, a mixture of contemporary and historical references.

'It's absolutely necessary to tell a story that has something to do with us – isn't that much more important than the actual story of Hans Böhm? ... The film shows how and why a revolution fails' –RWF.

1970: *Der amerikanische Soldat (The American Soldier)*
d/sc–RWF. ph–Dietrich Lohmann. b&w. ed–Thea Eymèsz. des–Kurt Raab, RWF. m–Peer Raben; the song 'So Much Tenderness' by RWF and Peer Raben, sung by Günther Kaufmann. l.p–Karl Scheydt (*Ricky*), Elga Sorbas (*Roas*), Jan George (*Jan*), Margarethe von Trotta (*Maid*), Hark Bohm (*Doc*), Ingrid Caven (*Singer*), Eva Ingeborg Scholz (*Ricky's Mother*), Kurt Raab (*Ricky's Brother*), Marius Aicher (*Cop*), Gustl Datz (*Police Chief*), Marquand Bohm (*Private Detective*), RWF (*Franz*), Katrin Schaake (*Magdalena Fuller*), Ulli Lommel (*Gypsy*), Irm Hermann (*Whore*). p.c–anti-teater. 35 mm. 80 mins.

German-born Ricky returns to Munich from America (and service in Vietnam), and is hired by three cops to carry out a series of murders. Between killings he rejoins his old friend Franz, and visits his mother and brother; Rosa von Praunheim, girlfriend of one of the cops, falls in love with him. Ricky kills Rosa, and he and Franz face a final showdown with the police in the railway station. Both are gunned down.

The film is constructed as a collage of references to his own and others' work: names, characters, situations and visual details evoke other films from *Gods of the Plague* to Sam Fuller's *Pickup on South Street*. There is even a reference forward: in a direct-to-camera monologue, the hotel maid recounts what will become the story for *Fear Eats the Soul*, albeit with a different (and more cynical) ending.

1970: *Warnung vor einer heiligen Nutte (Beware of a Holy Whore)*
'Motto: Pride Comes Before a Fall'
d/sc–RWF. ph–Michael Ballhaus. col. ed–Franz Walsch, Thea Eymèsz. des–Kurt Raab. m–Peer Raben, Gaetano Donizetti, Elvis Presley, Ray Charles, Leonard Cohen, Spooky Tooth. l.p–Lou Castel (*Jeff*), Eddie Constantine (*Himself*), Hanna Schygulla (*Hanna*), Marquand Bohm (*Ricky*), RWF (*Sascha*), Ulli Lommel (*Korbinian*), Katrin Schaake (*Scriptgirl*), Benjamin Lev (*Candy*), Monika Teuber (*Billi*), Margarethe von Trotta (*Production Secretary*), Gianni di Luigi (*Cameraman*), Rudolf Waldemar Brem (*Lighting Electrician*), Herb Andress (*Coach*), Thomas Schieder (*Jesus*), Kurt Raab (*Fred*), Hannes Fuchs (*David*), Marcella Michelangeli (*Margret*), Ingrid Caven (*Extra*), Harry Baer (*Her Husband*), Magdalena Montezuma (*Irm*), Werner Schroeter (*Deiters*), Karl Scheydt, Tanja Constantine, Maria Novelli, Enzo Monteduro, Achmed Em Bark, Michael Fengler, Burghard Schlicht, Dick Randall, Peter Berling, Tony

Bianchi, Renato dei Laudadio, Gianni Javarone, Peter Gauhe, Marcello Zucche. p.c–anti-teater-X-film/Nova International (Rome). 35 mm. 103 mins.

In a hotel on the Spanish coast, the cast and crew of a film await the arrival of their director Jeff, their star Eddie Constantine, and the German production money. Jeff arrives to find everything in chaos and struggles to impose some order. Eventually shooting begins.

'*Beware of a Holy Whore* is the frank recapitulation of the shooting of *Whity*. Those who were there can recognise almost all the things which have since become anecdotes. The head, the energy, the sexuality is, naturally, the director: Lou Castel donned Fassbinder's leather jacket and starts acting like a young Brando ... The realisation of fantasy in the film is secondary to the attempts to work things out with oneself and others, the image has nothing to do with the reality of those producing it ... The film that's supposed to be made is about state-sanctioned violence, but those making it can't cope with the small everyday violence that forms human relationships or tears them apart' – Wolfgang Limmer, *Süddeutsche Zeitung*.

'*Beware of a Holy Whore* is specifically about the situation of trying to live and work as a group' – RWF.

1970: *Pioniere in Ingolstadt (Pioneers in Ingolstadt)*
d–RWF. sc–RWF, from the play by Marie Luise Fleisser. ph–Dietrich Lohmann. col. ed–Thea Eymèsz. des–Kurt Raab. m–Peer Raben. l.p–Hanna Schygulla (*Berta*), Harry Baer (*Karl*), Irm Hermann (*Alma*), Rudolf Waldemar Brem (*Fabian*), Walter Sedlmayr (*Fritz*), Klaus Löwitsch (*Sergeant*), Günther Kaufmann (*Max*), Carla Aulaulu (*Frieda*), Elga Sorbas (*Mariel*), Burghard Schlicht (*Klaus*), Gunther Krää (*Gottfried*). p.c–anti-teater/Janus Film und Fernsehen (for ZDF). 35 mm. 87 mins.

Fleisser's play has been transposed from the Twenties to the present day. Soldiers stationed in Ingolstadt have essentially transient affairs with local girls. Alma resigns herself to promiscuity, but the waitress Berta believes she has found a lasting relationship with Karl. She is, however, mistaken.

The final *anti-teater* film has been widely attacked as RWF's most perfunctory and least engaged work. 'The play has a simple social logic: soldiers have to be brutal, superficial lovers because their profession makes them that ... Fassbinder's film has a complicated unlogic – because its absurd changes and additions to the original destroy the social context.' – Benjamin Henrichs, *Fernsehen und Film*.

1971: *Der Händler der vier Jahreszeiten (The Merchant of Four Seasons)*
d/sc–RWF. ph–Dietrich Lohmann. col. ed– Thea Eymèsz. des–Kurt Raab. m–archive selections; the song 'Buona Notte' by Rocco Granata. l.p–Hans Hirschmüller (*Hans Epp*), Irm Hermann (*Irmgard Epp*), Hanna Schygulla (*Anna*), Andrea Schober (*Renate Epp*), Gusti Kreissl (*Hans' Mother*), Heide Simon (*Heide*), Kurt Raab (*Kurt*), Klaus Löwitsch (*Harry*), Karl Scheydt (*Anzell*), Ingrid Caven (*Hans' 'Great Love'*), Peter Chatel (*Doctor*), Lilo Pempeit (*Customer*), Walter Sedlmayr (*Man who sells cart*), El Hedi Ben Salem (*Moroccan*), Hark Bohm (*Policeman*), Michael Fengler (*Playboy*), RWF (*Zucker*), Elga Sorbas (*Marile Kosemund*), Daniel Schmid, Harry Baer and Marian Seidowski (*Job Applicants*). p.c–Tango Film. 35 mm. 89 mins.

Would-be engineer and ex-foreign legionnaire Hans Epp, oppressed by his mother and rejected by his one 'great love' on grounds of class, enters a loveless marriage with Irmgard and sets up as a fruit and vegetable vendor. After Irmgard tries to leave him, he suffers a heart attack and grows increasingly depressed about his life. A row with his family drives him out into a bar, where he drinks himself to death.

The film's title is a literal translation of the French 'marchand des quatre saisons' (= street vendor), and sounds as odd in German as it does in English.
'It's a story that almost everyone I know has lived himself. A man wishes that he had made something of his life that he never did. His education, his environment, his circumstances don't admit the fulfilment of his dream' – RWF.

1972: *Die bitteren Tränen der Petra von Kant (The Bitter Tears of Petra von Kant)*
'Dedicated to the one who here became Marlene'
d/sc–RWF, based on his own play. ph–Michael Ballhaus. col. ed–Thea Eymèsz. des–RWF. m–The Platters, The Walker Brothers, Giuseppe Verdi. l.p–Margit Carstensen (*Petra von Kant*), Hanna Schygulla (*Karin Thimm*), Irm Hermann (*Marlene*), Eva Mattes (*Gabriele von Kant*), Katrin Schaake (*Sidonie von Grasenabb*), Giselda Fackeldey (*Valerie von Kant*). p.c–Tango Film. 35 mm. 124 mins.
Once widowed, once divorced, fashion designer Petra von Kant lives with her factotum, Marlene. A friend's chance introduction of another girl, Karin, leads Petra into a lesbian affair with the vaguely sluttish ingénue, until Karin's husband returns to Europe and she rushes to rejoin him. Petra lapses into extreme self-pity. After passing through a serious breakdown, she offers the hitherto ignored Marlene a new warmth. Marlene promptly leaves her.
'I don't find it a particularly theatrical film. The thing is that the woman in it places herself in a theatrical kind of situation ... everyone has experienced pain in love, and has wished (naturally enough) for a greater love than it was possible to have. Most people suffer because they are incapable of really expressing their grief' – RWF.

1972: *Wildwechsel*
d–RWF. sc–RWF, from the play by Franz Xaver Kroetz. ph–Dietrich Lohmann. col. ed–Thea Eymèsz. des–Kurt Raab. m–Ludwig van Beethoven. l.p–Jörg von Liebenfels (*Erwin*), Ruth Drexel (*Hilda, his Wife*), Eva Mattes (*Hanni, their Daughter*), Harry Baer (*Franz*), Rudolf Waldemar Brem (*Dieter*), Hanna Schygulla (*Doctor*), Kurt Raab (*Boss*), Karl Scheydt and Klaus Löwitsch (*Policemen*), Irm Hermann and Marquand Bohm (*Police Officials*), El Hedi Ben Salem (*Friend*). p.c–Intertel (for SFB). 35 mm. 102 mins.
The 14-year-old Hanni meets and sleeps with the 19-year-old worker Franz. A jealous friend of Hanni's reports their affair, and Franz is arrested for seducing a minor. Paroled for good behaviour, he resumes his liaison with Hanni, more secretively than before. When Hanni becomes pregnant, she urges him to kill her father, so that they can marry. But Franz is arrested for the murder; Hanni visits him in jail and tells him that she has had a miscarriage. Widely attacked after its TV premiere, not least by Franz Xaver Kroetz, author of the original play, who called RWF's attitude to the characters 'obscene'. The film subsequently ran into further trouble from the censor board, who demanded the elimination of a close-up of a penis before permitting theatrical showings.
'Everything in the film is also in the original play' – RWF.

1972: *Acht Stunden sind kein Tag (Eight Hours are not a Day)*
'A Family Series'
Part 1: *Jochen and Marion;* part 2: *Oma and Gregor;* part 3: *Franz and Ernst;* part 4: *Harald and Monika;* part 5: *Irmgard and Rolf.*
d/sc–RWF. ph–Dietrich Lohmann. col. ed–Marie Anne Gerhardt. des–Kurt Raab.

m–Jean Gepoint (=Jens Wilhelm Petersen). *l.p.*–Gottfried John (*Jochen*), Hanna Schygulla (*Marion*), Luise Ullrich (*Oma*), Werner Finck (*Gregor*), Anita Bucher (*Käthe*), Wolfried Lier (*Wolf*), Christine Oesterlein (*Klara*), Renate Roland (*Monika*), Kurt Raab (*Harald*), Andrea Schober (*Sylvia*), Thorsten Massinger (*Manni*), Irm Hermann (*Irmgard Erlkönig*), Wolfgang Zerlett (*Manfred*), Wolfgang Schenck (*Franz*), Herb Andress (*Rüdiger*), Rudolf Waldemar Brem (*Rolf*), Hans Hirschmüller (*Jürgen*), Peter Gauhe (*Ernst*), Grigorios Karipidis (*Giuseppe*), Karl Scheydt (*Peter*), Victor Curland (*Master Kretzschmer*), Rainer Hauer (*Gross*), Margit Carstensen, Christianne Jannessen, Doris Mattes, Gusti Kreissl and Lilo Pempeit (*Housewives in Part 2*), Katrin Schaake, Rudolf Lenz and Jörg von Liebenfels (*Landlords in Part 2*), Ulli Lommel, Ruth Drexel, Walter Sedlmayr, Helga Feddersen, Heinz Meier, Karl-Heinz Vosgerau, Peter Chatel, Valeska Gert, Eva Mattes, Marquand Bohm, Klaus Löwitsch, Hannes Gromball, Peter Märthesheimer. *p.c*–WDR. 16 mm. Part 1: 101 mins., part 2: 100 mins., part 3: 92 mins., part 4: 88 mins., part 5: 89 mins. (all at 25 f.p.s.).

The lives at home and at work of the Krüger family, their in-laws, friends and colleagues. Shown on German TV at monthly intervals, but WDR discontinued the series after five episodes, on the grounds that the scripts for the remaining three were less 'entertaining'.

'We wanted to say that trade unions are something that no longer have anything at all to do with people, that if they could do anything for people really then they'd have to go back to fundamentals. That's an example of something that one isn't allowed to say so simply and straightforwardly, probably. And all these things together, that's to say on the one hand the increasing dramatic complexity and the way that things get more problematic, and on the other the on-going political element (but always very human, always seen from a very human level), these were undoubtedly what decided them to cancel it' – RWF.

1973: *Welt am Draht*
d–RWF. *sc*–Fritz Müller-Scherz, RWF, based on the novel by Daniel F. Galouye. *ph*–Michael Ballhaus. *col*. *ed*–Marie Anne Gerhardt. *des*–Kurt Raab. *m*–Gottfried Hüngsberg, plus archive selections. *l.p*–Klaus Löwitsch (*Fred Stiller*), Mascha Rabben (*Eva*), Adrian Hoven (*Vollmer*), Ivan Desny (*Lause*), Barbara Valentin (*Gloria*), Karl-Heinz Vosgerau (*Siskins*), Günter Lamprecht (*Wolfgang*), Margit Carstensen (*Schmidt-Gentner*), Wolfgang Schenck (*Hahn*), Joachim Hansen (*Edelkern*), Rudolf Lens (*Hartmann*), Kurt Raab (*Holm*), Karl Scheydt (*Lehner*), Rainer Hauer (*Stuhlfaut*), Ulli Lommel (*Rupp*), Heinz Meier (*Weinlaub*), Peter Chatel (*Hirse*), Ingrid Caven, Eddie Constantine, Gottfried John, Elma Karlowa, Christine Kaufmann, Rainer Langhans, Bruce Low, Karsten Peters, Katrin Schaake, Walter Sedlmayr, El Hedi Ben Salem, Christiane Maybach, Rudolf Waldemar Brem, Peter Kern, Ernst Küsters, Peter Moland, Doris Mattes, Liselotte Eder, Solange Pradel, Maryse Delannoy, Werner Schroeter, Magdalena Montezuma, Corinna Brocher, Peter Gauhe, Dora Karras-Frank. *p.c*–WDR. 16 mm. Part 1: 99 mins., part 2: 101 mins. (at 25 f.p.s.).

When Vollmer, head of a cybernetic institute that produces forecasts of future political and economic developments, commits suicide under mysterious circumstances, his friend and colleague Stiller begins an investigation of his own. He grows involved with Vollmer's daughter Eva. Gradually he discovers that the world he inhabits is not real, but a computerised projection from the real world; Eva herself reveals that she is merely a projection of the real Eva elsewhere. The police hunt down and shoot Stiller, but he is 'saved' by Eva, who transfers his consciousness to another world.

Widely compared with Godard's *Alphaville* in Germany, because of the similarities of theme, method and the underlying evocations of the Hollywood private eye.

1973: *Angst essen Seele auf (Fear Eats the Soul)*
d/sc–RWF. ph–Jürgen Jürges. col. ed–Thea Eymèsz. des–RWF. m–archive selections. l.p–Brigitte Mira (*Emmi*), El Hedi Ben Salem (*Ali*), Barbara Valentin (*Barbara*), Irm Hermann (*Krista*), RWF (*Eugen*), Karl Scheydt (*Albert*), Elma Korlowa (*Mrs. Kargus*), Anita Bucher (*Mrs. Ellis*), Gusti Kreissl (*Paula*), Walter Sedlmayr (*Grocer*), Doris Mattes (*His Wife*), Liselotte Eder (*Mrs. Münchmeyer*), Marquand Bohm (*Gruber*), Hannes Gromball (*Head Waiter*), Katherina Herberg (*Girl in Bar*), Rudolf Waldemar Brem (*Man in Bar*), Peter Moland (*Boss of Garage Workshop*), Margit Symo (*Hedwig*), Peter Gauhe (*Bruno*), Helga Ballhaus (*Yolanda*). p.c–Tango Film. 35 mm. 93 mins.

Emmi, a widowed German charwoman of around 60, meets Ali, a Moroccan immigrant labourer many years her junior. Their lonelinesses match, and they succumb to an impulse to marry. But their union brings out all the latent fear, prejudice and snobbery in those around them, and by the time that the social order has returned to 'normal', the marriage itself is falling prey to the very same symptoms.

The English title somewhat misrepresents the original, in that 'Angst essen Seele auf' (spoken in the film by Ali) is pidgin-German, and strikes the ear of a native speaker very strangely.

The plot, already introduced in the maid's monologue in *The American Soldier*, corresponds quite closely with that of Douglas Sirk's 1955 *All That Heaven Allows*. 'It's just a matter of a similar story; the films are products of different circumstances. Sirk's is a kind of fairytale; mine is too, but one from everyday life. Sirk had the courage simply to tell the story. I probably didn't trust myself to simply do that. But I'd been wanting to do it for years ... I didn't have an actress for it until I met Brigitte Mira. It's a story of two people who are in practically the same situation, who have much the same motives for repressing themselves' – RWF.

1973: *Martha*
d/sc–RWF. ph–Michael Ballhaus. col. ed–Liesgret Schmitt-Klink. des–Kurt Raab. m–archive selections. l.p–Margit Carstensen (*Martha Hyer*), Karlheinz Böhm (*Helmut Salomon*), Gisela Fackeldey (*Mother*), Adrian Hoven (*Father*), Barbara Valentin (*Marianne*), Ingrid Caven (*Ilse*), Ortrud Beginnen (*Erna*), Wolfgang Schenck (*Boss*), Günter Lamprecht (*Dr. Salomon*), Peter Chatel (*Kaiser*), El Hedi Ben Salem (*Hotel Guest*), Kurt Raab (*Secretary*), Rudolf Lenz (*Porter*). p.c–WDR. 16 mm. 112 mins.

After her father's sudden death on holiday in Rome, Martha Hyer meets and soon marries Helmut Salomon, encouraged by her mother. She tries to conform in every way to Helmut's expectations, but gradually realises that his demands are essentially sadistic. She flees the house, crashes her car and is crippled; Helmut collects her from the hospital in her wheelchair, saying that she is now his forever.

'Martha is really not oppressed, but rather educated. And this education is like an oppression. If Martha at the end of the film is no longer among the living, then she's reached what she most deeply wanted ... In fact, the film tells a story that goes like this: What makes this woman happy? Most men can't oppress as perfectly as women would like' – RWF.

1974: *Fontane Effi Briest (Effi Briest)*
'or, Many who have an inkling of their possibilities and needs none the less accept the

prevailing order in their head in the way that they act, and thereby strengthen and confirm it absolutely'
d–RWF. *sc*–RWF, based on the novel by Theodor Fontane. *b&w*. *ed*–Thea Eymèsz. *des*–Kurt Raab. *m*–motif by Camille Saint-Saens. *l.p*–Hanna Schygulla (*Effi Briest*), Wolfgang Schenck (*Baron Geert von Instetten*), Karlheinz Böhm (*Wüllersdorf*), Ulli Lommel (*Major Crampas*), Ursula Strätz (*Roswitha*), Irm Hermann (*Johanna*), Lilo Pempeit (*Luise von Briest*), Herbert Steinmetz (*Effi's Father*), Hark Bohm (*Chemist Gieshübler*), Rudolf Lenz (*Rummschüttel*), Barbara Valentin (*The Singer Marietta Tripelli*), Karl Scheydt (*Kruse*), Theo Tecklenburg (*Pastor Niemeyer*), Barbara Lass (*Polish Cook*), Eva Mattes (*Hulda*), Andrea Schober (*Annie*), Anndorthe Braker (*Mrs Pasche*), Peter Gauhe (*Dagobert*). *voices* – Hanna Schygulla, Wolfgang Schenck and Karlheinz Böhm speak with their own voices; other parts are dubbed as follows: Ulli Lommel by Wolfgang Hess, Hark Bohm by Kurt Raab, Ursula Strätz by Renate Küster, Herbert Steinmetz by Fred Maire, Lilo Pempeit by Rosemarie Fendel, Irm Hermann by Margit Carstensen. *narrator*–RWF. *p.c*–Tango Film. 35 mm. 141 mins.

The 17-year-old Effi Briest is married by her parents to the much older Baron von Instetten. She is dissatisfied by the match, and lonely in her new home, but too inexperienced to know why. She forms a fleeting liaison with her husband's friend Major Crampas. Von Instetten discovers it six years later: he duels with and kills Crampas, and separates himself from Effi, keeping custody of their daughter Annie. A year later, Effi dies.

'Everything that I've earned in the last three or four years went into *Effi Briest*, and I don't expect the film to earn it back, I just have to earn the opportunity through the film to get it back elsewhere. (...) I made *Effi Briest* because Fontane's attitude to his society was a lot like my own, and I'm a German, making films for German audiences' –RWF.

1975: *Faustrecht der Freiheit (Fox)*
'For Armin and all the others'
d–RWF. *sc*–RWF, Christian Hohoff. *ph*–Michael Ballhaus. *col. ed*–Thea Eymèsz. *des*–Kurt Raab. *m*–Peer Raben. *l.p*–RWF (*Franz Biberkopf – 'Fox'*), Peter Chatel (*Eugen*), Karlheinz Böhm (*Max*), Adrian Hoven (*Eugen's Father*), Ulla Jacobsen (*Eugen's Mother*), Harry Baer (*Philip*), Christiane Maybach (*Hedwig*), Peter Kern (*Florist*), Brigitte Mira (*Shopowner*), Karl Scheydt (*Sideshow Manager*), Irm Hermann (*Stripper*), Kurt Raab (*Barman*), Walter Sedlmayr (*Car Dealer*), Hans Zander, Ursula Strätz, Elma Karlowa, Barbara Valentin, Bruce Low, Evelyn Künneke, Ingrid Caven, Marquand Bohm, Liselotte Eder. *p.c*–Tango Film. 35 mm. 123 mins.

Out of work after his fairground sideshow has been closed by the police, Franz Biberkopf is picked up in a public lavatory by antique dealer Max, who introduces him to Eugen. Franz and Eugen become lovers; Franz wins half a million DM in the national lottery and supports both Eugen himself and his family business, a printing works. When Franz' money is exhausted, Eugen rejects him and returns to his former lover Philip. Franz, brokenhearted, dies of an overdose of tranquillisers.

'I think it's incidental that the story happens among gays. It could have worked just as well in another milieu. But I rather think that people look back at it more carefully precisely because of its setting, because if it had been a "normal love affair", then the melodramatic aspect would have loomed much larger. I think that a moment comes when people stop noticing that they're watching gays, but then they're going to ask themselves: what have we just been watching? We've seen a story that took place among people whom we in fact consider unnatural. And through such bewilderment, through a moment of positive shock, the whole story also looks different' –RWF.

1975: *Mutter Küsters Fahrt zum Himmel (Mother Küsters' Trip to Heaven)*
d–RWF. *sc*–RWF, Kurt Raab. *ph*–Michael Ballhaus. *col. ed*–Thea Eymèsz. *des*–Kurt Raab. *m*–Peer Raben. *l.p*–Brigitte Mira (*Mother Küsters*), Karlheinz Böhm (*Thälmann*), Margit Carstensen (*Mrs. Thälmann*), Ingrid Caven (*Corinna Corinne*), Armin Meier (*Ernst*), Irm Hermann (*Helene*), Gottfried John (*Journalist*), Peter Kern (*Nightclub manager*), Peter Chatel and Peter Bollag (*Photographers*). *p.c*–Tango Film. 35 mm. 91 mins. (New ending shot and added November 1975).

Harassed by pressmen after her husband has killed one of his bosses and committed suicide at work, Mother Küsters is briefly consoled by her son Ernst and daughter, cabaret singer Corinna. But Ernst and his wife move away and Corinna uses the scandal to further her career, and Mother Küsters turns to the communist Thälmann couple for advice and help in clearing her late husband's name. But her new-found left-wing friends prove as spineless and mendacious as the rest.

Turned down by the 1975 Berlin Festival, and disrupted by left-wing protests at its 'fringe' screening in the Berlin Forum, the original version of RWF's film (with its overtly tragic ending) created more furore in Germany than any of his previous films. The new ending, with Mother Küsters finding consolation from the person of an equally lonely night-watchman, remains highly ironic in its effect: its absurd fortuitousness merely underlines the essential tragedy of the story.

1975: *Angst vor der Angst (Fear of Fear)*
d–RWF. *sc*–RWF, based on an idea by Asta Scheib. *ph*–Jürgen Jürges, Ulrich Prinz. *col. ed*–Liesgret Schmitt-Klink, Beate Fischer-Weiskirch. *des*–Kurt Raab. *m*–Peer Raben. *l.p*–Margit Carstensen (*Margot*), Ulrich Faulhaber (*Kurt*), Brigitte Mira (*Mother*), Irm Hermann (*Lore*), Armin Meier (*Karli*), Adrian Hoven (*Dr. Merck*), Kurt Raab (*Neighbour Bauer*), Ingrid Caven (*Edda*), Lilo Pempeit (*Mrs. Schall*), Helga Märthesheimer (*Dr. von Unruh*), Herbert Steinmetz (*Dr. Auer*), Hark Bohm (*Dr. Rozenbaum*), Constanze Haas (*Bibi*). *p.c*–WDR. 16 mm. 88 mins.

Seemingly happily married housewife Margot is troubled by inexplicable fears during a pregnancy. Hostility from her mother and sister, incomprehension from her husband Kurt and a curious sense of empathy with a suicidal neighbour, Bauer, all intensify her depression. The nearby chemist Merck prescribes her valium, and she has a brief affair with him. But she turns to drink, and then suffers a breakdown. When Kurt collects her from the hospital some time later, she seems recovered, but she returns home to find that Bauer has finally killed himself.

A kind of companion piece to the previous TV film with Margit Carstensen, *Martha*, but with the pressures on the central character being more explicitly internal.

'If the film has a terrible conclusion, an ending that you can't live with, you must find something else. Death is emancipation ... not in the sense that the word is commonly used, but emancipation meaning that the protagonist, representing the audience, learns that a utopia is necessary. They need it.' – RWF.

1976: *Ich will doch nur, dass Ihr mich liebt (I Only Want You to Love Me)*
d–RWF. *sc*–RWF, drawn from one of the interviews in the book *Lebenslänglich* by Klaus Antes and Christiane Ehrhardt. *ph*–Michael Ballhaus. *col. ed*–Liesgret Schmitt-Klink. *des*–Kurt Raab. *m*–Peer Raben. *sound*–Karsten Ullrich. *assistant d*–Renate Leiffer, Christian Hohoff. *producer*–Peter Märthesheimer. *l.p*–Vitus Zeplichal (*Peter*), Elke Aberle (*Erika*), Alexander Allerson (*Father*), Ernie Mangold (*Mother*), Johanna Hofer (*Grandmother*), Katharina Buchhammer (*Ulla*), Wolfgang Hess (*Construction*

Supervisor), Armin Meier (*Site Foreman*), Erika Runge (*Interviewer*), Ulrich Radke (*Erika's Father*), Annemarie Wendl (*Erika's Mother*), Janos Gönczöl (*Bar Landlord*), Edith Volkmann (*Bar Landlady*), Robert Naegele (*Court Bailiff*), Axel Ganz (*Housemaster*), Inge Schultz (*Frau Emmerich*), Heinz H. Bernstein (*Furniture Salesman*), Helga Bender (*Boutique Salesgirl*), Adi Gruber (*Post Office Clerk*), Sonja Neubauer (*Jewellery Salesgirl*), Heide Ackermann (*Sewing Machine Saleswoman*), Reinhard Brex (*Building Contractor*). p.c–Bavaria Atelier, for WDR. 16 mm. 104 mins. (at 25 f.p.s.).

Peter spends his adolescence feeling profoundly neglected by his parents. After marrying his childhood sweetheart Erika, he moves away from home and settles in a flat in a large town with his wife. His modest wages can barely keep pace with the demands of his new home and his wife – and, soon, of their child. The pressures finally drive him crazy: he commits a 'senseless' murder, and is given a ten-year prison sentence for manslaughter. Based on an authentic case-history, this is one of Fassbinder's most simple and personal works in its portrayal of the violent consequences of a lack of love.

'In this film I've imagined that there's no love between the parents, so where would they find the love to give their child? They don't reckon with love, only with money.' – RWF.

1976: *Satansbraten* (*Satan's Brew*)
'Ce qui différence les païens de nous, c'est qu'à l'origine de toutes leurs croyances, il y a un terrible effort pour ne pas penser en hommes, pour garder le contact avec la création entière, c'est-à-dire avec la divinité – Antonin Artaud'

d/sc–RWF. ph–Jürgen Jürges (first 14 days, October 1975), Michael Ballhaus (last 15 days, January–February 1976). col. ed–Thea Eymèsz, Gabi Eichel. des–Kurt Raab, Ulrike Bode. m–Peer Raben. sound–Paul Schöler, Rolf-Peter Notz, Roland Henschke. assistant d–Ila von Hasperg, Christa Reeh, Renate Leiffer. producer–Michael Fengler. l,p–Kurt Raab (*Walter Kranz*), Margit Carstensen (*Andrée*), Helen Vita (*Luise Kranz*), Volker Spengler (*Ernst*), Ingrid Caven (*Lilly*), Marquand Bohm (*Rolf, her husband*), Ulli Lommel (*Lauf*), Y Sa Lo (*Lana*), Katharina Buchhammer (*Irmgart von Witzleben*), Armin Meier (*Stricher*), Vitus Zeplichal (*Urs*), Dieter Schidor (*Willy*), Peter Chatel (*Eugen*), Michael Octave (*Junger*), Katren Gebelein (*Lilly's Mother*), Helmut Petigk (*Schneider*), Hannes Gromball (*Taxi Driver*), Adrian Hoven (*Doctor*), Monika Teuber (*Woman in Lift*). p.c–Albatros Produktion, for Trio Film. 35 mm. 112 mins.

Blocked writer Walter Kranz, once a 'poet of the revolution', begins to reproduce the writings of Stefan George. He decides to pose as George reincarnate, and hires a coterie of homosexuals to attend his poetry readings. Meanwhile his long-suffering wife and halfwit brother Ernst try to lead their 'normal' lives regardless. Kranz attracts a disciple in the person of librarian Andrée, demands money from his penniless parents, kills a rich woman for her money. A prostitute whom he tries to blackmail turns out to be respectably middle-class; when her protector beats him up, Kranz discovers that he enjoys pain.

'Kranz is someone who finds it possible to realise that he has little to say. He doesn't digest, he lives and re-lives situations. Like most people, he never grows up. It was clear from the beginning that the film would be a comedy.' – RWF.

'All my films, or nearly all of them, have been shown on German TV, generally two years after theatrical release. *Satan's Brew* is the only one that won't be shown. That's the one that they'll never accept.' – RWF.

1976: *Chinesisches Roulette* (*Chinese Roulette*)
d/sc–RWF. *ph*–Michael Ballhaus. *col. ed*–Ila von Hasperg, Juliane Lorenz. *des*–Kurt Raab, Peter Muller, Helga Ballhaus. *m*–Peer Raben. *sound*–Wolfgang Hoffmann, Roland Henschke. *assistant d*–Ila von Hasperg. *producers*–RWF, Jean-François Stévenin. *l.p*–Margit Carstensen (*Ariane Christ*), Andrea Schober (*Angela Christ*), Ulli Lommel (*Kolbe*), Anna Karina (*Irene*), Macha Méril (*Traunitz*), Alexander Allerson (*Gerhard Christ*), Volker Spengler (*Gabriel*), Brigitte Mira (*Kast, his mother*), Armin Meier (*Petrol Pump Attendant*), Roland Henschke (*Beggar*). *p.c*–Albatros Produktion/Les Films du Losange (Paris). 35 mm. 86 mins.

Businessman Gerhard Christ and his wife Ariane are tricked by their handicapped daughter Angela into arriving simultaneously at their country house with their respective lovers; Angela herself also arrives, with her dumb nurse Traunitz. The ensuing social embarrassments climax in a game of 'Chinese roulette', after which Ariane shoots Traunitz. Then another shot is heard...

'I thought to myself, how come this married couple both have long-term extra-marital affairs? I hit on the idea that they had problems with their child. These led them to want out of their marriage – not right out, but certainly to want to evade it somehow. So I settled on the child as an idea. Then I thought that, to pose a real threat, the child would have to be more intelligent than anyone else – which is just what physically weak children are.' – RWF.

1977: *Bolwieser*
d–RWF. *sc*–RWF, based on the novel by Oskar Maria Graf. *ph*–Michael Ballhaus. *col. ed*–Ila von Hasperg, Juliane Lorenz. *des*–Kurt Raab, Nico Kehrhan. *m*–Peer Raben. *sound*–Reinhard Gloge. *assistant d*–Christian Hohoff, Ila von Hasperg, Udo Kier. *production supervisor*–Willi Segler, Herbert Knopp. *l.p*–Kurt Raab (*Xaver Ferdinand Maria Bolwieser, Station Master*), Elisabeth Trissenaar (*Hanni*), Bernhard Helfrich (*Frank Merkl*), Udo Kier (*Schafftaler*), Volker Spengler (*Mangst*), Armin Meier (*Scherber*), Karl-Heinz von Hassel (*Windegger*), Gustl Maryhammer (*Neidhart, Hanni's Father*), Maria Singer (*Frau Neidhart*), Willi Harlander (*Stempflinger*), Hannes Kaetner (*Lederer*), Gusti Kreissl (*Frau Lederer*), Helmut Alimonta (*Hartmannseder*), Peter Kern (*Treuberger*), Gottfried John (*Finkelberger*), Gerhard Zwerenz (*Ferryman*), Helmut Petigk (*Innkeeper*), Sonja Neudorfer (*Innkeeper's Wife*), Monika Teuber (*Mariele*), Nino Korda (*Lawyer*), Hannes Gromball (*Judge in District Court*), Alexander Allerson (*Chairman*), Manfred Gunther (*Defendant*), Roland Henschke (*Judge in Werburg*), Adolph Gruber (*Accused Peasant*), Doris Mattes (*Witness*), Ulrich Radke (*Counsel Schneider*), Liselotte Pempeit (*Frau Käser*), Reinhard Weiser (*Sailerbub*), Elma Karlowa (*Nurse*), Isolde Barth and Margot Mahler (*Taxi-dancers*), Renate Muhri (*Prostitute*), Monica Gruber (*Waitress*), Katharina Buchhammer (*Barmaid*). *p.c*–Bavaria Atelier, for ZDF. 16 mm. Part 1: 104 mins.; Part 2: 96 mins.

Bavaria in the 1920s. Happily married station master Bolwieser returns from a tour of duty to find that his wife Hanni unjustly suspects him of infidelity. Soon after, Hanni launches into an affair with her former schoolmate Merkl, known to everyone in the small community but her husband. The issue eventually comes to court, and Bolwieser perjures himself to protect his wife. When the latter transfers her affections to the hairdresser Schafftaler, Merkl has his revenge by indicting Bolwieser for perjury. Bolwieser is jailed; Hanni divorces him and marries Schafftaler. On his release, Bolwieser becomes a ferryman.

RWF intended to re-edit the film into a version lasting about 100 minutes for cinema release, but had to drop the plan for legal reasons. Oskar Maria Graf's little-remembered novel *Bolwieser – Roman eines Ehemanns* was published in 1931, two years before Graf fled from the Nazis to America. The book carries the following motto: 'The human condition: instability, weariness, fear'.

1977: *Frauen in New York* (*Women in New York*)
d–RWF. *sc*–the play *The Women* by Clare Booth, translated into German by Nora Gray. *ph*–Michael Ballhaus. *col. ed*–Wolfgang Kerhutt. *des*–Rolf Glittenberg. *sound*–Horst Faahs. *production supervisor*–Dieter Meichsner. *l.p*–Christa Berndl (*Mary, Mrs. Stephen Haines*), Margit Carstensen (*Sylvia, Mrs. Howard Fowler*), Anne-Marie Kuster (*Peggy, Mrs. John Day*), Eva Mattes (*Edith, Mrs. Phelps Potter*), Angela Schmid (*Nancy Blake/Princess Tamara/Miss Trimmerback*), Heide Grübl (*Jane/Gymnastics Teacher/Doubtful Girl*), Ehmi Bessel (*Mrs. Wagstaff/Ingrid, the cook/First Manageress/Miss Watts/Second Lady*), Susanne Werth (*First Hairdresser/First Salesgirl/First Girl*), Carola Schwarz (*Second Hairdresser/Second Salesgirl/Helene, the maid*), Irm Hermann (*Olga, the manicurist/Miriam*), Adelheid Muther (*Euphie/Model/Cigarette-girl*), Ilse Bally (*Mud-pack/Second Manageress/First Lady*), Andrea Grosske (*Miss Fordyce, the tutor/Luca, the cleaning woman/Maggie, the cook/Widow*), Christina Prior (*Little Mary*), Gisela Uhlen (*Mrs. Moorehead/Countess de Lage*), Barbara Sukowa (*Crystal Allen*), Henny Zschoppe (*Nurse/Sadie, the hat-check girl*), Sabine Wegener (*Debutante*). *p.c*–NDR. 16 mm. 111 mins. (at 25 f.p.s.)

A film version of a play Fassbinder directed in Hamburg, Clare Booth Luce's *The Women*. It gave Fassbinder an opportunity to indulge his passion for working with women – there are forty women in the play and no men. The play dates from the 1930s, and Fassbinder was accused by the critics of being anti-women (a frequent criticism of late). As usual, he chose to work *against* the text, and from this has constructed an entertaining and engaging play about love between upper-class women with nothing better to do than sneer at others when things go wrong with their lives and loves.

1977: *Eine Reise ins Licht – Despair* (*Despair*)
'Dedicated to Antonin Artaud, Vincent Van Gogh, Unica Zürn.'
d–RWF. *sc*–Tom Stoppard, based on the novel by Vladimir Nabokov. *ph*–Michael Ballhaus. *col. ed*–Reginald Beck, Juliane Lorenz. *des*–Rolf Zehetbauer, Herbert Strabel, Jochen Schumacher. *m*–Peer Raben. *sound*–James Willis, John Stevenson, Milan Bor. *assistant d*–Harry Baer, Stefen Zurcher. *producer*–Peter Märthesheimer. *l.p*–Dirk Bogarde (*Hermann Hermann*), Andréa Ferreol (*Lydia Hermann*), Volker Spengler (*Ardalion*), Klaus Löwitsch (*Felix Weber*), Alexander Allerson (*Mayer*), Bernhard Wicki (*Orlovius*), Peter Kern (*Muller*), Gottfried John (*Perebrodov*), Adrian Hoven (*Inspector Schelling*), Roger Fritz (*Inspector Braun*), Hark Bohm (*Doctor*), Voli Geiler (*Madam*), Hans Zander (*Muller's Brother*), Y Sa Lo (*Elsie*), Liselotte Eder (*Secretary*), Armin Meier (*Worker in Hermann's Factory/Twins in the film-within-the-film*), Gitti Djamal (*Woman in Pension*), Ingrid Caven (*Hotel Receptionist*), Isolde Barth. *p.c*–NF Geria II/SFP (Paris), for Bavaria Atelier. 35 mm. 119 mins. Shot in English.

Berlin, 1930. Russian émigré chocolate manufacturer Hermann Hermann, feeling increasingly dislocated from his marriage and his work and increasingly ill-at-ease in his social environment, happens upon the tramp Felix Weber, whom he believes to be his perfect double. Hermann decides to exchange identities with Weber, intending to kill him and start a new life with the insurance money. Weber is eventually persuaded

115

to agree to the substitution, and is promptly shot by Hermann. The latter flees to Switzerland to await his wife. When the police (guided by Lydia Hermann) arrive to arrest him, they find that Hermann has completely lost his sanity.

'The film is dedicated to Artaud, Van Gogh and Zürn because all three were people who could be happy in their madness, until they killed themselves. I don't really know, but I think that they lived a very private utopia in their madness. My Hermann Hermann is free. He *chooses*. Did Artaud and Van Gogh choose? I don't know, and there's no way I can know for sure. I can only guess. It's a hypothesis.' – RWF.

1978: *Deutschland im Herbst* (*Germany in Autumn*)
Fassbinder's episode:
d/sc–RWF. *ph*–Michael Ballhaus. *col*. *ed*–Juliane Lorenz. *sound*–Roland Henschke. *l.p.*–RWF, Armin Meier, Lilo Pempeit [Liselotte Eder].
26 mins.

Other episodes:
d–Alf Brustellin, Alexander Kluge, Maximiliane Mainka, Edgar Reitz, Katja Rupé/Hans Peter Cloos, Volker Schlöndorff, Bernhard Sinkel. *sc*–the directors, Heinrich Böll, Peter Steinbach. *ph*–Jürgen Jürges, Bodo Kessler, Dietrich Lohmann, Colin Mounier, Jörg Schmidt-Reitwein. *col & b&w*. *ed*–Heidi Genée, Mulle Goetz-Dickopp, Beate Mainka-Jellinghaus, Tanja Schmidbauer, Christina Warnck. *des*–Henning von Gierke, Winfried Hennig, Toni Lüdi. *sound*–Martin Müller, Günter Stadelmann. *producers*–Theo Hinz, Eberhard Junkersdorff. *production managers*–Heinz Badewitz, Karl Helmer, Herbert Kerz. *l.p*–Hannelore Hoger, Katja Rupé, Hans Peter Cloos, Angela Winkler, Franzisca Walser, Vadim Glowna, Helmut Griem, Dieter Last, Enno Patalas, Mario Adorf, Horst Mahler, Wolf Biermann, Manfred Rommel, Wolfgang Bachler, Heinz Bennent, Joachim Bissmeyer, Joey Buschmann, Caroline Chaniolleau, Otto Friebel, Hildegard Friese, Michael Gahr, Horatius Heberle, Petra Kiener, Lisa Mangold, Eva Meier, Franz Priegel, Werner Possardt, Leon Rainer, Walter Schmiedinger, Gerhard Schneider, Corinna Spies, Eric Vilgertshofer, Manfred Zapatka, members of the Rote Rübe Collective. *p.c*–Pro-ject Filmproduktion im Filmverlag der Autoren/Hallelujah Film/Kairos Film. 35 mm. 123 mins. (when premiered at the Berlin Film Festival in 1978: 134 mins.).

A collective reflection on the state of the West German nation at the time of the *Berufsverbot* legislation and in the wake of the Baader-Meinhof deaths in Stammheim Prison, comprising both fictional and documentary sequences. RWF's contribution cross-cuts between two domestic situations: (1) RWF returns to his apartment in Munich from a trip to Paris, to work on his script for the projected film adaptation of *Berlin Alexanderplatz*. He is greeted and ministered to by his lover Armin Meier (dedicatee of *Fox* and supporting player in most of RWF's films from 1975 to his suicide in 1978), but RWF repeatedly picks quarrels with Meier over the political crises caused by the Mogadishu hijacking and the deaths in Stammheim. At one point RWF orders some cocaine to boost his spirits, but flushes it down the toilet when he fears a police raid on the apartment. (2) RWF has a kitchen-table discussion with his mother Liselotte Eder about the political situation. Ms. Eder evinces orthodox bourgeois outrage at the tactics of the terrorists; RWF agitatedly points out the flaws and holes in her reasoning.

RWF's episode could broadly be compared with Godard's contribution to *Loin du Vietnam*, inasmuch as both are predicated on their directors' anguish at their own impotence in the face of national and international events. RWF, however, is at pains to dramatise (= externalise) his personal anxieties: he presents himself both as a 'concerned' individual and as a domestic tyrant, taking out his own insecurities on his long-suffering lover.

1978: *Die Ehe der Maria Braun* (*The Marriage of Maria Braun*)
'For Peter Zadek.'
d–RWF. sc–Peter Märthesheimer, Pea Fröhlich, from an idea by RWF. ph–Michael Ballhaus. col. ed–Juliane Lorenz. des–Helga Ballhaus, Norbert Scherer. m–Peer Raben. sound–James Willis. assistant d–Rolf Bührmann. l.p–Hanna Schygulla (*Maria Braun*), Klaus Löwitsch (*Hermann Braun*), Ivan Desny (*Oswald*), Gottfried John (*Willi*), Gisela Uhlen (*Mother*), Gunter Lamprecht (*Wetzel*), George Byrd (*Bill*), Elisabeth Trissenaar (*Betti*), Isolde Barth (*Vevi*), Peter Berling (*Bronski*), Sonja Neudorfer (*Red Cross Nurse*), Liselotte Eder (*Frau Ehmke*), Volker Spengler (*Schaffner*), Karl-Heinz von Hassel (*Public Prosecutor*), Michael Ballhaus (*Lawyer*), Christine Hopf-de Loup (*Notary*), Hark Bohm (*Senkenberg*), Dr. Horst-Dieter Klock (*Man with Car*), Günther Kaufmann (*Man on the Train*), Bruce Low (*Man at the Conference*), RWF (*Tradesman*), Claus Holm (*Doctor*), Anton Schirsner (*Grandpa Berger*), Hannes Kaetner (*Registrar*), Martin Häussler (*Reporter*), Norbert Scherer, Rolf Bührmann and Arthur Glogau (*Prison Guards*). p.c–Albatros Produktion. 35 mm. 98 mins.

Maria and Hermann Braun marry during an air-raid, just before Hermann is sent off to fight on the Russian front. After the war he is missing, presumed dead, and Maria sets up home with a black GI. But Hermann reappears: in a fight, the GI is killed (by Maria), and Hermann takes the blame and goes to jail. While he serves his time, Maria takes up with a wealthy industrialist and saves the money he showers on her. On his release, Hermann proudly refuses her help and emigrates to Canada, where he makes his fortune. Maria stays with the industrialist, and inherits his wealth when he dies. Hermann returns to Germany, but Maria's feelings towards him have changed; no sooner are they reunited than their house explodes . . .

'I think that marriage is a kind of living together, something that's needed and necessary – if you're raised the way we were raised. I find that marriage is something artificial. In regard to marriage, I make my films so that people who are married or perhaps have a marriage on the rocks can see them and review their own marriage concretely. For example, I think it's much more positive if a film of mine helps a marriage to fall apart when it's failing already than it would be to leave the institution of marriage unquestioned, unexamined.' – RWF (in *Germany in Autumn*)

1978: *In einem Jahr mit 13 Monden* (*In a Year with 13 Moons*)
d/sc/ph–RWF. col. camera assistant–Werner Lüring. ed–RWF. des–Franz Vacek. m–Peer Raben. sound–Karl Scheidt, Wolfgang Mund. collaborators–Milan Bor, Walter Bockmayer, Jo Braun, Juliane Lorenz, Volker Spengler, Alexander Witt. production manager–Isolde Barth. l.p–Volker Spengler (*Elvira Weishaupt*), Ingrid Caven (*Red Zora*), Gottfried John (*Anton Seitz*), Elisabeth Trissenaar (*Irene*), Eva Mattes (*Marie-Ann*), Günther Kaufmann (*Chauffeur*), Lilo Pempeit (*Sister Gudrun*), Isolde Barth (*Sybille*), Karl Scheidt (*Hacker*), Walter Bockmayer (*Seelenfrieda*), Peter Kollek (*Drunk*), Bob Dorsay (*Man in the Street*), Günther Holzapfel (*Clerk*), Ursula Lillig (*Cleaning Woman*), Gerhard Zwerenz (*Burghard Hauer, the author*). p.c–Tango Film/Pro-ject Filmproduktion im Filmverlag der Autoren. 35 mm. 124 mins.

The last five days in the life of the transexual Elvira Weishaupt, who is driven to suicide by the hostility of those around her. A series of encounters with old friends and former lovers leads her to look back over her unhappy life as a man and as a woman.

'1. Every 7th year is a Year of the Moon. Certain people, whose existence is predominantly determined by their feelings, are afflicted by unusually severe depressions in these Moon Years, comparable with those they suffer in years with 13 new moons, albeit less intense. And if a Moon Year coincides with a year of 13 new moons, they can often suffer major personal disasters. In the 20th century, there are six years when this dangerous conjunction occurs: one of them is 1978. Previous ones have been 1908, 1929, 1943 and 1957. After 1978, the year 1992 will again jeopardise the existence of many a human being.

2. The film *In a Year with 13 Moons* describes a person's encounters during the last five days of his life, and attempts to determine – through these encounters – whether this one person's decision not to carry on beyond this last day, the fifth, should be rejected, at least understood, or maybe even found acceptable.

3. The film is set in Frankfurt, a place whose particular structure virtually provokes biographies like this one – or at least doesn't make them seem particularly unusual. Frankfurt is not a haven of friendly mediocrity, not a place where opposites are squared off against each other, not peaceful, not fashionable or nice; on the contrary, Frankfurt is a town where you run into all the general contradictions of society at every street-corner, incessantly. Or at least, if you don't stumble over *them* immediately, the contradictions that are being fairly successfully ironed out everywhere else.' – RWF.

1979: *Die 3. Generation* (*The Third Generation*)
'Dedicated to a true lover – and hence, probably, to nobody?'
d/sc/ph–RWF. *col. ed*–Juliane Lorenz. *des*–Raul Gimenez, Volker Spengler. *m*–Peer Raben. *sound*–Milan Bor, Jean-Luc Marié. *technical collaborators*–Ekkehard Heinrich, Hans Bücking, Wolfgang Rühl. *assistant d*–Diana Elephant. *production manager*–Harry Baer. *l.p*–Volker Spengler (*August Brem*), Bulle Ogier (*Hilde Krieger*), Hanna Schygulla (*Susanne Gast*), Harry Baer (*Rudolf Mann*), Vitus Zeplichal (*Bernhard von Stein*), Udo Kier (*Edgar Gast*), Margit Carstensen (*Petra Vielhaber*), Günther Kaufmann (*Franz Walsch*), Eddie Constantine (*Peter Lenz*), Raul Gimenez (*Paul*), Y Sa Lo (*Ilse Neumann*), Hark Bohm (*Gerhard Gast*), Claus Holm (*Grandpa Gast*), Lilo Pempeit (*Mother Gast*), Jürgen Draeger (*Hans Vielhaber*). *p.c*–Tango Film/Pro-ject Filmproduktion im Filmverlag der Autoren. 35 mm. 111 mins.

'A comedy in six parts, about party games, full of suspense, excitement and logic, horror and madness, just like the fairy stories they tell children, to make the life which ends in death more endurable.' – RWF.

'*The Third Generation* could mean: the German middle class between 1848 and 1933, our grandfathers and how they experienced the Third Reich and what they remember of it, our fathers who, after the war, had the opportunity to build a nation which could have been more human and free than any that had gone before, and what this opportunity subsequently disintegrated into.

But *The Third Generation* could also mean: the present generation of terrorists, if we accept the notion that there have already been first and second generations. The first would have been those whose mixture of idealism and almost pathological despair at their own impotence within the system finally drove them virtually insane. And the second would have been those whose understanding of their predecessors' motives led them to defend its representatives – often enough literally, in that many of them were lawyers. But this defence became so arduous, and was so rapidly slandered as a 'criminal' activity, that this generation was driven to follow its predecessors into the underground.

Whatever approximation of understanding an individual may be prepared to extend to the actions and motives of these first and second generations, any attempt to comprehend the motives of the third generation is more than difficult. It seems to me that the third generation of terrorists has less in common with its predecessors than it has with this society and the power that it wields, whoever that power may benefit. I have become convinced that they do not know what they are doing, that the only sense that can be found in their actions lies in the act itself, the pseudo-adventure of taking on the system...

This phenomenon, which exists exclusively in West Germany, has a great deal to do with this country, with its faults and failures, with the democracy that it received and (like a gift-horse) refused to look in the mouth. Our democracy is based on fundamental values which can degenerate all too easily into taboos – which the state then blindly defends against its own citizenry, this state which is becoming just a little more totalitarian with each passing day. What a godsend this terrorism must be to this state in its present stage of development. If these terrorists did not exist, this state would have to invent them. Perhaps it even has?

The Third Generation is not a so-called political film, except in the sense that every film is political. I considered myself indebted to several other films when I made it: *Touch of Evil* by Orson Welles, *Flamingo Road* by Michael Curtiz, and *Conversation Piece* by Luchino Visconti.' – RWF (abridged from a slightly longer statement)

Video Productions as director

1970: *Das Kaffeehaus (The Coffee-Shop)*
d–RWF, from the stage production by RWF, Peer Raben and *anti-teater*. *sc*–RWF, based on the play by Carlo Goldoni. *ph*–Dietbert Schmidt, Manfred Förster. b&w. *des*–Wilfried Minks. *m*–Peer Raben. *l.p*–Margit Carstensen (*Vittoria*), Ingrid Caven (*Placida*), Hanna Schygulla (*Lisaura*), Kurt Raab (*Don Marzio*), Harry Baer (*Eugenio*), Hans Hirschmüller (*Trappolo*), Günther Kaufmann (*Leander*), Peter Moland (*Pandolfo*), Wil Rabenauer (*Ridolfo*). *p.c*–WDR. 105 mins.

1972: *Bremer Freiheit (Bremen Freedom)*
d–RWF, Dietrich Lohmann. *sc*–RWF. *ph*–Dietrich Lohmann, Hans Schugg, Peter Weyrich. col. *ed*–Friedrich Niquet, Monika Solzbacher. *des*–Kurt Raab. *m*–archive selections. *l.p*–Margit Carstensen (*Geesche*), Ulli Lommel (*Miltenberger*), Wolfgang Schenck (*Gottfried*), Walter Sedlmayr (*Priest*), Wolfgang Kieling (*Timm*), Rudolf Waldemar Brem (*Bohm*), Kurt Raab (*Zimmermann*), Fritz Schediwy (*Johann*), Hanna Schygulla (*Luise Maurer*), RWF (*Rumpf*), Lilo Pempeit (*Mother*). *p.c*–Telefilm Saar (for SR). 87 mins.

1973: *Nora Helmer*
d–RWF. *sc*–RWF, based on the play *A Doll's House* by Henrik Ibsen, translated into German by Bernhard Schulze. *ph*–Willi Raber, Wilfried Mier, Peter Weyrich, Gisela Loew, Hans Schlugg. col. *ed*–Anne-Marie Bornheimer, Friedrich Niquet. *des*–Friedhelm Boehm. *m*–archive selections. *l.p*–Margit Carstensen (*Nora*), Joachim Hansen (*Torvald*), Barbara Valentin (*Mrs. Linde*), Ulli Lommel (*Krogstedt*), Klaus Löwitsch (*Dr. Rank*), Lilo Pempeit (*Marie*), Irm Hermann (*Helene*). *p.c*–Telefilm Saar (for SR). 101 mins.

1975: *Wie ein Vogel auf dem Draht (Like a Bird on the Wire)*
d–RWF. *sc*–RWF, Christian Hohoff, Anja Hauptmann, *musical d*–Kurt Edelhagen. col. *ed*–Helga Egelhofer. *des*–Kurt Raab. *with*–Brigitte Mira, Evelyn Künneke.

Films as scriptwriter

1969: *Fernes Jamaica (Distant Jamaica)*
d–Peter Moland. *sc*–RWF. *ph*–Herbert Paetzold. *b&w*. *l.p*–Katrin Schaake, Ulli Lommel, Hannes Gromball, Ingrid Caven, William Powell. *p.c*–anti-teater. 35 mm. 14 mins.

1976: *Schatten der Engel (Shadow of Angels)*
d–Daniel Schmid. *sc*–RWF, Daniel Schmid, based on RWF's play *Der Müll, die Stadt und der Tod, oder Frankenstein am Main*. *ph*–Renato Berta. *col*. *ed*–Ila von Hasperg. *sound*–Günther Kortwich. *producers*–Michael Fengler, Jordan Bojilov. *l.p*–Ingrid Caven, RWF, Klaus Löwitsch. *p.c*–Albatros Produktion/Artcofilm (Geneva). 35 mm. 105 mins.

Films (other than his own) as actor

1967: *Tony Freunde* (*d*–Paul Vasil. as Mallard)
1968: *Der Bräutigam, die Komödiantin und der Zuhalter* (*The Bridegroom, the Comedienne and the Pimp*) (*d*–Jean-Marie Straub. as The Pimp)
1969: *Alarm* (*d*–Dieter Lemmel. as the man in uniform)
Al Capone im deutschen Wald (*d*–Franz Peter Wirth. as Heini)
Baal (*d*–Volker Schlöndorff. as Baal)
Frei bis zum nächsten Mal (*d*–Korbinian Köberle. as the mechanic)
1970: *Matthias Kneissl* (*d*–Reinhard Hauff. as Flecklbauer)
Der plötzliche Reichtum der armen Leute von Kombach (*The Sudden Good Fortune of the Poor People of Kombach*) (*d*–Volker Schlöndorff. as a peasant)
Supergirl (*d*–Rudolf Thome. as the man who looks through window)
1973: *Zärtlichkeit der Wölfe* (*The Tenderness of Wolves*) (*d*–Ulli Lommel. as Wittkowski.)
1974: *1 Berlin-Harlem* (*1 Single, Berlin to Harlem*) (*d*–Lothar Lambert. as himself)
1976: *Schatten der Engel* (*Shadow of Angels*) (*d*–Daniel Schmid. as the pimp, Raoul)
1978: *Bourbon Street Blues* (*d*–Douglas Sirk. Short, based on the one-act play by Tennessee Williams)

Bibliography

Fassbinder's Published Writing
The following list is not exhaustive, and most notably omits several journalistic essays published in West German newspapers.

Liebe ist kälter als der Tod. Script of the film. Published in the magazine *Film*, no. 8, 1969.
Antiteater. Contains the plays *Katzelmacher, Preparadise sorry now* and *Die Bettleroper.* Published by Suhrkamp Verlag, Frankfurt am Main, as edition suhrkamp no. 443, 1973.
Imitation of Life: Über die Filme von Douglas Sirk. Essay on six films by Sirk. Published in the magazine *Fernsehen und Film*, no. 2, 1971. An English translation

by Thomas Elsaesser has been published in the book *Douglas Sirk*, edited by Laura Mulvey and Jon Halliday and published by Edinburgh Film Festival, 1972. The translation has also been printed in *New Left Review*, no. 91, May–June 1975.

Antiteater 2. Contains the plays *Das Kaffeehaus, Bremer Freiheit* and *Blut am Hals der Katze*. Published by Suhrkamp Verlag as edition suhrkamp no. 560, 1974.

... Schatten freilich und kein Mitleid – Ein paar ungeordnete Gedanken zu Filmen von Claude Chabrol. Short polemical essay, critical of Chabrol. Published in the book *Reihe Film 5: Claude Chabrol*, edited by Peter W. Jansen and Wolfram Schütte, published by Carl Hanser Verlag, Munich, as Reihe Hanser 190. Translated into English by Derek Prouse as *Insects in a Glass Case*, and published in *Sight and Sound*, Autumn 1976.

Schatten der Engel. Script of the film, identical with the play as published in *Stücke 3*, below. Published by Verlag 2001, Frankfurt am Main, 1976.

Stücke 3. Contains the plays *Das brennende Dorf, Die bitteren Tränen der Petra von Kant* and *Der Müll, die Stadt und der Tod*. Published by Carl Hanser Verlag as Theaterbuch 1, 1978.

Record

Antiteater's Greatest Hits. Compilation of musical and verbal extracts from *antiteater* plays and films, selected by Peer Raben. Includes the songs from *Whity* and *The American Soldier*. Issued on the Kuckuck label, no. 2640 102, 1973.

Criticism

Reihe Film 2: Rainer Werner Fassbinder, edited by Peter W. Jansen and Wolfram Schütte, published by Carl Hanser Verlag, Munich. (3rd edition, 1979). Remains the definitive source of information about all RWF's film and early theatre work; Peter Iden's essay in the present publication is translated from this book, and the filmography above is greatly in debt to its 'Daten' section by Hans Helmut Prinzler. It contains an exhaustive list of reviews of individual RWF films. (In German)

I Fassbinders Spejl, by Christian Braad Thomsen, published by Fremads Fokusbøger, Copenhagen, 1975. A painstaking survey of all RWF's work in film and theatre up to 1975. (In Danish)

Film Comment, vol. 11, no. 6, Nov–Dec. 1975. Special sections on RWF and Douglas Sirk, including an abridgement of RWF's essay on Sirk and articles by Manny Farber and Patricia Patterson, Roger Greenspun, John Hughes and James McCourt.

Positif, no. 183/4, July–August 1976. Special issue on melodrama; includes an article on RWF, a complete translation into French of RWF's essay on Sirk, and versions of four of the interviews with RWF by Christian Braad Thomsen in the present publication. (In French)

Film Quarterly, vol. 30, no. 2, Winter 1976/7. Lengthy, sympathetic, middlebrow account of RWF's films up to *Mother Küsters* by Paul Thomas. Occasionally erroneous in matters of fact and translation.

Cahiers du cinéma, no. 275, April 1977. Concise, hostile analysis of the 'Fassbinderian cybernetic' by Serge Daney. (In French)

Jump Cut, no. 16, 1977. The special 'Gay Men and Film' section reprints a polemical exchange of views on *Fox* between Bob Cant and Andrew Britton, from the English magazine *Gay Left*.

La Revue du cinéma – Image et son, no. 333, November 1978. Chronology of RWF's work, with a simple analysis by Daniel Sauvaget. (In French)

Interviews
This highly selective list of published interviews includes all the texts quoted in the notes to the filmography under individual film titles. See also the brief list of interviews appended to Thomas Elsaesser's article *A Cinema of Vicious Circles*, above.

Filmkritik, no. 8, August 1969. (In German)
Ecran, no. 31, December 1974. (In French)
Cinéma'74, no. 193, December 1974. (In French)
Sight and Sound, vol. 44, no. 1, Winter 1974/5.
Film Comment, vol. 11, no. 6, November–December 1975.
Cineaste, vol. 8, no. 2, Autumn 1977.
Cinema, no. 2, 1978. (In German)
La Revue du cinéma – Image et son, no. 333, November 1978. (In French)

Other Material
Das bisschen Realität, das ich brauche. Wie Filme entstehen. Book on the craft of film-making by Hans Günther Pflaum, using examples from the shooting of *I Only Want You to Love Me*, *Satan's Brew* and *Chinese Roulette*. Interjections by RWF. Published by Carl Hanser Verlag, Munich, 1976. (In German).

Printed in Great Britain by Spottiswoode Ballantyne Ltd, Colchester and London

Advances in
ATOMIC, MOLECULAR, AND OPTICAL PHYSICS

VOLUME 56

Editors

ENNIO ARIMONDO
University of Pisa
Pisa, Italy

PAUL R. BERMAN
University of Michigan
Ann Arbor, Michigan

CHUN C. LIN
University of Wisconsin
Madison, Wisconsin

Editorial Board

P.H. BUCKSBAUM
SLAC
Menlo Park, California

M.R. FLANNERY
Georgia Tech
Atlanta, Georgia

C. JOACHAIN
Université Libre de Bruxelles
Brussels, Belgium

J.T.M. WALRAVEN
University of Amsterdam
Amsterdam, The Netherlands